Decades of our Lives

70s

Decades of our Lives

CLASSIC, RARE AND UNSEEN

70s

FROM THE ARCHIVES OF THE DAILY MAIL

Trans
Atlantic
Press

The new decade represented a reality check for the "peace and love" generation. Cambodia suffered from Pol Pot's murderous regime; Ugandan Asians were driven out by the equally unsavory Idi Amin; Bangladesh was born out of bloody internal conflict in Pakistan. The Middle East, Northern Ireland, and Cyprus were among the political powder kegs, and the world was rocked by an oil crisis. Vietnam ended in defeat for US forces; Soviet troops rolled into Afghanistan and would meet a similar fate.

America won the superpower battle waged on the chessboard, then lost its president over the Watergate scandal. Spitz and Korbut were the darlings of the Munich Olympics, but even this sporting jamboree fell victim to terror tactics.

Urban guerrilla groups such as Baader-Meinhof and the Red Brigade proliferated, while Iran ditched the Shah and staged an Islamic Revolution. Borg racked up four Wimbledon titles, Muhammad Ali's bee sting won him an unprecedented third heavyweight crown, and we could record their exploits on the new-fangled VCR.

From the momentous and the apocalyptic to the offbeat and the trivial, the photographs in this book, from the archives of the *Daily Mail*, chart the people, places, and events that made up a memorable decade.

The Isle of Wight pop festival
which took place over the
August Bank Holiday in 1970
attracted over a quarter of
a million fans. The five day
festival took place in sweltering
heat and many of the fans
headed for the coast to cool
off, chill out, and let it all hang
out. 1970 was the third and last
consecutive year of the festival
and it was the largest event of
its kind until the 1973 Summer
Jam at Watkins Glen, USA.

1970

OPPOSITE: American singer and guitarist Jimi Hendrix plays the Isle of Wight Festival, August 30, 1970. A few weeks later Hendrix was found dead in his girlfriend's apartment in Notting Hill, west London. There is still some controversy over his death but post-mortem results revealed that he had asphyxiated in his own vomit.

ABOVE: Elvis Presley in a scene from the documentary *That's the Way It Is*. The film showed him in rehearsals and the recording studio, as well as on stage, and included footage from the opening show of his first tour since 1957. Elvis had rarely performed live during the 1960s, concentrating instead on his career in Hollywood, but by 1970 he had returned to hits roots, appearing regularly at the International in Las Vegas and touring the USA.

ABOVE: On April 20, 1970, US President Richard Nixon appeared in a televised broadcast from "the Western White House," La Casa Pacifica in San Clemente, California, to announce plans for the withdrawal of an additional 150,000 US troops from South Vietnam, as part of his plan for "Vietnamization," which had begun the previous year. The aim was to increase the role of the South Vietnamese forces in the conflict while gradually decreasing the number of American troops in the region. However, at the end of the month Nixon sent American troops into Cambodia, provoking demonstrations in the US and heated debate in Congress.

OPPOSITE: A wounded American paratrooper awaits evacuation in Vietnam

1970

OPPOSITE: Willis Reed, number 19, with Red Holzman (right), head coach of the New York Knicks, is being interviewed by ABC's Howard Cosell after the Knicks, inspired by the presence of Reed, defeated the Los Angeles Lakers in game seven of the 1970 NBA Championship on May 8, 1970, at Madison Square Garden in New York City. The Knicks won the Championship four games to three.

RIGHT: Jochen Rindt, pictured with his wife Nina, after winning the British Grand Prix at Brands Hatch driving the ground-breaking Lotus 72. The 1970 season had started well but in practice at Monza, Italy, in September Rindt crashed into a barrier at high speed and was killed. Jochen Rindt became Formula One's first posthumous World Champion.

1970

ICHAEL NORMAN ANTIQUES LTD.

ABOVE: British skinheads running through the streets of Brighton chanting in support of their football team, Chelsea. The early 1970s saw the continuation of the skinhead fashion which had developed from the mods during the late 1960s. At first the look was defined by short hair—a feather cut often with a razor parting. The mods' parka was replaced by the Crombie overcoat. The music they danced to was Jamaican ska and reggae.

OPPOSITE: Pop group Slade, one of the early "glam rock" groups in the 1970s, had a string of hits including "Cum on Feel the Noize," "Mama Weer All Crazee Now," and "Merry Christmas Everybody." This photograph, taken in 1970, shows Noddy, Don, Dave, and Jimmy in their skinhead days, the UK inner city fashion before glam rock.

ABOVE: Australian singer Olivia Newton-John and American Ben Thomas rehearsing together during the making of the movie *Toomorrow*. The film was intended by Don Kirshner, creator of the Monkees, to launch an eponymous band into stardom. Newton-John went on to star with John Travolta in the hit film *Grease* released in 1978.

OPPOSITE: In the comedy movie *There's a Girl in my Soup*, directed by Roy Boulting, celebrity chef and serial womanizer Peter Sellers encounters gorgeous Goldie Hawn on the bounce from breaking up with her English rock-musician boyfriend. Sellers was the comedy genius of his generation and Goldie a gifted comedienne who rose to fame via *Rowan & Martin's Laugh-In*—the cult 1960s comedy show from downtown Burbank. While Hawn frequently portrayed the typical dumb blonde, her acting career and her abilities as a dancer and singer would prove her all-round talent.

1970

A typing pool, showing women engaged in secretarial work. Jobs for women were still somewhat limited at the dawn of the 1970s, although the feminist movement would experience a "second wave" in both Britain and the US throughout the decade, with women entering work in greater numbers and securing legal rights to equal pay.

The first Boeing 747 airliner touched down at London Heathrow: a Pan Am flight with 361 passengers on board, made up of airline staff and some families and officials of the American Federal Aviation Agency. Pilot Captain Jesse Tranter (center) and flight engineer Jake Nagle (left) are pictured with cabin crew beside the plane after landing.

1970

John Lennon and Yoko Ono (above) and Paul and Linda McCartney (opposite). Amidst rumor and speculation, Paul McCartney announced on April 10 that he was leaving the Beatles to follow his solo career, releasing his first album, *McCartney*, a week later, to be followed soon after by the prophetically titled Beatles album *Let It Be*. John Lennon had been pursuing his own agenda outside the Beatles for some time and although McCartney's announcement was unexpected, few were surprised. Although the Beatles were officially over as a band, both Lennon and McCartney, who had married their respective partners within days of each other the previous year, were very happy in their personal lives.

1970

ABOVE: The first Triumph Stag rolled off the production line in 1970: British Leyland matched Italian design with a powerful engine and construction to meet exacting US safety standards, aiming this modern thoroughbred squarely at the export market. However, fewer than 3,000 cars made it to the US. Although it was the sports car that everyone wanted to own, poor manufacturing and a number of design faults disappointed many owners of the 25,000 cars produced up to 1977. Current owners of these iconic cars have been able to remedy original design flaws and drive a more reliable car today than those that came off the original production line.

OPPOSITE: Strong patterns in bold colors were the theme of mid-1970s fashion—the model wears a print shirt in two different patterns from Clobber, with a butterfly leather belt and cream and orange silk scarf.

ABOVE: Gary Warren, Jenny Agutter, and Sally Thomsett in *The Railway Children*—a haunting and innocent drama set in Victorian England, telling the story of a family that falls on hard times yet manages to make a new life around the railway close to their new home. They avert a serious accident and their enterprise helps them unlock the mystery of their disappeared father. A critical success for Lionel Jeffries in his directorial debut, the movie also vindicated producer Bryan Forbes' financial guarantees backing Jeffries.

OPPOSITE: Revelers, including three men dressed as priests, at the first Glastonbury Festival, held on Worthy Farm, near Pilton, Somerset. The event was launched by farmer Michael Eavis as the Pilton Pop, Folk and Blues Festival, and attracted a crowd of just 1,500, with T-Rex as the headlining act. Today the Glastonbury Festival is one of the world's largest and longest-running outdoor music events.

ABOVE: May 4 was one of the USA's blackest days, when Ohio National Guardsmen fired 67 shots at unarmed student protesters on the campus of Kent State University. Four students were killed outright; two of them were not protesters but were walking between lectures. Nine more students were wounded by the gunfire. The protest arose from introduction of the military service draft and the US incursion into Cambodia, announced by President Nixon on April 30. Before the campus protest there had been civil disorder in the town and the mayor had declared a state of emergency, bringing in the National Guard. Following the shooting Kent State closed for six weeks and a nationwide student strike affected four million students, closing schools and colleges across the USA.

OPPOSITE: Prince Charles graduated from Cambridge and entered the Royal Navy, training to be a pilot and, later in his six-year naval career, to fly helicopters. The same year he joined the navy he met Camilla Shand at a polo match; with Charles' protracted absence romance could not flower: Camilla married Charles' friend Andrew Parker Bowles instead.

ABOVE: Wilfred Brambell and Harry H. Corbett, stars of the BBC sitcom *Steptoe and Son*. Originally produced in black and white from 1962 to 1965, the show returned in color in 1970, and ran for another four series until 1974, also spawning two spin-off movies and the highly successful US TV adaptation, *Sanford and Son*.

OPPOSITE: Michael Caine and Britt Eckland during the filming of the cult British movie *Get Carter*. Based on the 1969 novel *Jack's Return Home* by Ted Willis, the movie was initially criticized for its bleakness and violence, but has come to be seen as a classic within the gangster genre.

1970

ABOVE: Singer Lulu and husband Bee Gee Maurice Gibb, who has just shaved off his beard for a part in a musical. The Bee Gees were well established in the 1970s but hit the heights of fame with the songs they wrote for the film *Saturday Night Fever*, released in 1977, starring, John Travolta.

OPPOSITE: Singer Tina Turner sporting a leopard skin coat. Having supported the Rolling Stones in 1969, Ike and Tina Turner's popularity continued to grow into the 1970s, and in the first year of the decade they appeared on *The Ed Sullivan Show* to perform their version of "Proud Mary" which would prove to be a major hit in 1971.

Benny Hill was a reinvention of the music hall entertainer for the TV era. Best known for his knockabout comedy, double entendre, and sexual humor, Benny achieved popularity and cult following on both sides of the Atlantic. After an "on-off" career with the BBC, Hill was signed up to Thames TV in 1969 and broadcast until 1989, when his style was deemed inappropriate for more politically correct times. In the late 1970s Thames leased TV airtime on both coasts of the USA and broadcast toned-down material for more conservative audiences. So began his US following. Benny had many guest celebrities on his shows and he is pictured here with actresses Aimi MacDonald and Diana Coupland.

English cricketer Fred Trueman, the best-known fast-bowler of his generation, with members of the cast of the much-loved British TV sitcom *Dad's Army*, in November 1970. Known as Fiery Fred, Trueman could launch himself into furious bowling action that dominated the opposing batsman, making him the hardest working of bowlers. *Dad's Army* featured the antics of a platoon of the Home Guard in World War II and ran for nine series with 80 episodes. Seen here, left to right: Arthur Lowe, Arnold Ridley, Bill Pertwee, John Le Mesurier, Trueman, Clive Dunn, John Laurie, and James Beck.

LEFT: British tennis player Sue Barker aged 13. Barker's career included 15 singles and 16 doubles titles and a victory in the French Open in 1976. After retirement Sue Barker became one of the faces of BBC sport, presenting coverage of both tennis and athletics.

OPPOSITE: *I'm just telling it like it is*—so went legendary sportscaster Howard Cosell's catchphrase. Cosell was a trained lawyer who went full time as a radio sports commentator in the mid-50s, moving to become sports anchor for WABC-TV in New York in 1961. In 1970 he became presenter for *Monday Night Football*—the first midweek coverage to be given to football. No doubt his legal training affected his commentating, as he favored a more intellectual approach than the customary play-by-play commentary, delivered in his characteristic staccato vocal style. He is forever associated with commentary on great sporting moments, from the early fights of Cassius Clay through the shocking events of the Munich Olympics, even interrupting his show to announce on air the death of John Lennon.

LEFT: Model Felicity Devonshire seen wearing a see-through mini dress. The use of man-made fibers such as polyester became increasingly common and refined during the 1970s, although with the introduction of midi and maxi dresses, not all women's fashions were as revealing as that pictured. Felicity meanwhile would go on to star in a number of erotic comedies during the 1970s, before turning her hand to property management.

OPPOSITE: Fashionably attired DJ Noel Edmonds on his engagement to Gillian Slater in 1970. Having begun his broadcasting career at Radio Luxembourg two years earlier, Edmonds moved to Radio 1 in 1970, where he would initially enjoy a two hour Saturday afternoon show, before replacing Kenny Everett, who was sacked from his Saturday morning program after making comments about Mary Peyton, wife of the British Transport Minister.

1971

The Jackson Five, America's
band of singing brothers
From Gary, Indiana, hit fame
in the early 1970s. Pictured
from left to right are: Marlon,
Jackie, Tito, Jermaine, and
Michael, with nine-year-old
Randy in a straw hat At the
age of ten Michael Jackson
became the youngest singer
ever to top the charts. He led
the vocals on "I Want You
Back" which toppled Edison
Lighthouse's "Love Grows"
from the number one spot.
In 1970 the young pop stars
spent 13 weeks at number one
in the US singles charts with
their first four releases, selling
over 15 million copies.

1971

LEFT: The aftermath of the Ibrox Stadium disaster, showing the twisted metal handrails of Stairway 13, where 66 people lost their lives as they attempted to leave the stadium in Glasgow following a Rangers–Celtic soccer match on January 2, 1971. There was initial speculation that departing Rangers fans had turned around on the stairs in response to a last minute equalizer by Colin Stein, leading to a massive crush, although this theory was discredited by the official inquiry that followed.

OPPOSITE: George Best, still one of Manchester United's star players in the 1970s. Unfortunately his playboy lifestyle meant his career was not only marked by brilliant performances on the field but also by episodes of drunkenness when off the pitch.

1971

OPPOSITE: "Heeeeere's Johnny!" introduced NBC's *The Tonight Show Starring Johnny Carson* for 30 years from 1962. Carson's show ran every weeknight until 1972, when guest presenters released Carson on Monday nights. The guest host tradition was a regular event, with the likes of Woody Allen standing in. Carson was not just a host and commentator; his show shaped the society of his time and anybody who was anybody had to appear on it.

RIGHT: In 1971 Michael Parkinson became a household name in Britain with his chat show which occupied the late Saturday evening slot on BBC TV. *Parkinson* attracted celebrities from all walks of life and all corners of the world. The show spawned a host of imitations but often without the in-depth interviews that Parkinson managed to conduct with his hallmark charm and candor. After its first run ended in 1982 the show was revived in 1998 and ran until 2007.

ABOVE: Children playing with "Klackers," a craze that swept across playgrounds throughout the US and Europe during the early 1970s. Consisting of two plastic balls attached to a length of cord, which could be made to click together, the toys were quickly banned by numerous schools after reports of injuries, ranging from bruising to broken bones.

OPPOSITE: A young dancer on *Top of the Pops* demonstrates the fashion of 1971: hot pants and thigh-high boots.

LEFT: Long distance runner David Bedford. In 1971 Bedford scored a victory in the International Cross Country Championships held in Spain, and went on to secure his first British record in the 3,000m steeplechase. He would however finish a disappointing sixth in the 10,000m final at the European Championships, having led the pack for much of the race. Ten years later, Bedford took part in the first London Marathon, and today he is director of the race.

OPPOSITE: Golfing champion Lee Trevino displays his score sheet after winning the British Open Championship at Birkdale in 1971. The same year he beat Jack Nicklaus to win the US Open and was awarded PGA Player of the Year.

OPPOSITE: Singer-songwriter Cat Stevens. Although he had enjoyed earlier successes, 1971 was a breakthrough year for Stevens, particularly in the US, where he would enjoy his first major hits with the singles "Wild World," "Moon Shadow," and "Peace Train," while the LPs *Tea for the Tillerman* and *Teaser and the Firecat* would attain gold record status on both sides of the Atlantic. Stevens converted to Islam in 1977, adopting the name Yusuf Islam the following year.

RIGHT: Swiss-born actress Ursula Andress made her name as Honey Rider in the 1962 James Bond Movie *Dr. No*. In 1971 she was to feature in *Soleil Rouge* (Red Sun) with Charles Bronson, a western-cum-samurai movie featuring the legendary Japanese actor Toshiro Mifune.

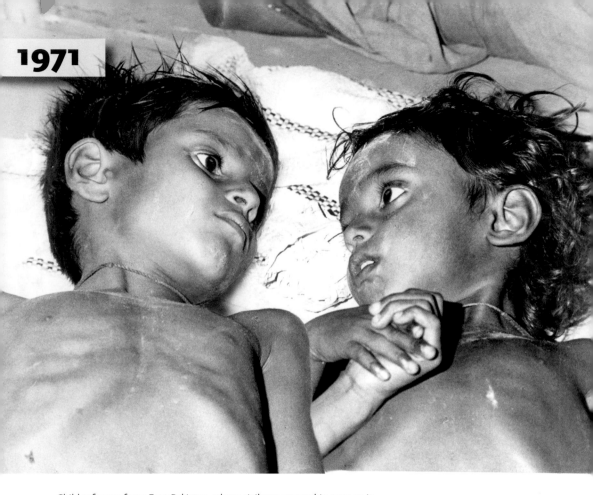

Child refugees from East Pakistan, where civil war erupted in 1971 as it sought independence from West Pakistan. The violence led to a serious humanitarian crisis, with millions of refugees crossing the border into India. With the assistance of Indian forces, East Pakistan gained its independence by the end of the year, taking the name Bangladesh. The devastation brought by the conflict was compounded by starvation and cholera outbreaks as the monsoon rains brought severe flooding to the region.

The Roman Catholic nun Mother Teresa, pictured distributing gifts in a leper colony in Calcutta, India, where she worked caring for the poor and sick. Although she had established the Missionaries of Charity religious order in 1950, it was during the 1970s that she came to wide public attention, largely on account of Malcolm Muggeridge's 1971 book, *Something Beautiful for God*. After her death in 1997 she was beatified by Pope John Paul II and given the title Blessed Teresa of Calcutta.

OPPOSITE: Fashionable "Kodak Girls" display their wares at the 1971 Ideal Home Exhibition, which showcased new advances in design and technology that were aimed at the domestic consumer. Meanwhile, that same year would see the development of the Sony Umatic and Philips video cassette recorders, the production of the world's first single-chip microprocessor, and the sending of the first electronic mail.

RIGHT: Movie star Ann-Margret arrived in London with her husband, Roger Smith, for the London premiere of the movie *Carnal Knowledge* in which she featured with Candice Bergen, Jack Nicholson, and Art Garfunkel. She received an Oscar nomination for her performance.

ABOVE: Scottish actor Sean Connery as James Bond, the British secret agent 007, in *Diamonds are Forever,* Connery's sixth and last Bond movie. For many Bond fans, Connery is the most convincing portrayal of the action hero.

OPPOSITE: Gene Hackman in character as Popeye Doyle in the classic 1971 crime movie *The French Connection*. The screenplay was based on real-life characters and situations in New York's Police Department. Directed by William Friedkin, the exhilarating movie was R-rated but that didn't stop it from winning five Oscars and receiving three further nominations.

American musician Frank Zappa outside the Albert Hall in London with his rock band The Mothers of Invention. With a busy European tour planned, including numerous UK dates, many concerts had to be canceled after Zappa was attacked by a crazed fan during their performance at the newly opened Rainbow Theatre, London, on December 10. Zappa fell from the stage and was badly injured, spending the next year in a wheelchair.

1971

OPPOSITE: British Prime Minister Edward Heath bids farewell to President Nixon following a two day conference in Bermuda. Against a backdrop of unrest in the Middle East, and the outbreak of civil war in Pakistan, the two leaders met to discuss such issues as international security and economics. Despite reports of broad agreement, the meeting was seen to mark the end of the "special relationship" between Britain and the US, as Heath looked to strengthen economic ties with Europe.

ABOVE: Indian troops advance unopposed into Bangladesh in December 1971 following the unconditional surrender of Pakistan's army.

OPPOSITE: Cybill Shepherd is captured here in her debut role as Jacy Farrow, starring opposite Jeff Bridges in *The Last Picture Show*. Peter Bogdanovich's first big movie grabbed two Oscars and a further six nominations for his depiction of growing up in America in the early 1950s. Based on an autobiographical novel by Larry McMurtry, the movie was shot in black and white and its soundtrack was composed completely from pop music. As well as established actors, Bogdanovich used lesser known names, including Randy Quaid, for whom this was also a film debut.

RIGHT: In 1971 Dustin Hoffman was on track to become one of the leading actors of his generation, first appearing as fictional pop composer Georgie Soloway in the quirky *Who Is Harry Kellerman and Why Is He Saying Those Terrible Things About Me?*, followed by his role in Sam Peckinpah's highly controversial *Straw Dogs*, in which he played David Sumner, a mild academic forced to fight for his life. Filmed on location in England, the movie was later banned under 1980s legislation in the UK for its depiction of rape and violence.

1971

OPPOSITE: Footballer George Best has his shirt pulled by Fred Callaghan during a match between Manchester United and Fulham in 1971. Widely regarded as one of the most naturally gifted footballers of all time, by 1971 Best's drinking and womanizing were beginning to overshadow his talents on the pitch, and he would be briefly suspended by his club for failing to attend a match against Chelsea. Despite this he continued to score numerous goals, including a cheeky, and famously disallowed, goal against England at Belfast's Windsor Park.

RIGHT: Model Shakira Baksh, aged 24. Born in Guyana, South America, but of Indian descent, Shakira initially aspired to become a fashion designer, before finding fame as a Miss World contestant in 1967. She went on to launch a modeling career in London during the early 1970s, and in 1973 married actor Michael Caine, with whom she would appear in the movie *The Man Who Would Be King*.

ABOVE: The "Fight of the Century" in Madison Square Garden between Joe Frazier, the reigning heavyweight champion, and ebullient challenger Muhammad Ali, attracted a live audience of over 20,000 with millions more watching on television around the world. Nobody could predict the outcome—it was Ali's speed and agility against Frazier's awesome power. What was certain for both fighters was their guaranteed purse of $2.5m each—at that time a record amount. However, a heavy blow from Frazier in the 15th round put Ali on his back and victory was declared for Frazier.

OPPOSITE: Ali combines family duties with his training schedule, by doing his road work while pushing his twin daughters, Rasheeda and Jamillah.

An American mortar team fires 60mm shells against Vietcong in support of US marines under attack. In late 1971, peace proposals were being exchanged between the belligerents; US forces were consolidating and adopting a more defensive role with greater focus on air-strikes.

The break-up of the Beatles left George Harrison (right) free to pursue his own interests. Inpired by the philosphy and music he had studied in India, George spent time with sitar player Ravi Shankar (left). Earlier in the year, George had started work on his solo album, *All Things Must Pass*, recorded at Abbey Road Studios and produced by Phil Spector.

ABOVE: In 1971 Charles Manson was sentenced to life imprisonment for his part in the brutal murder of actress Sharon Tate. Members of his cult known as "the Family," visciously slaughtered Sharon and four of her friends after they broke into the home she shared with husband, Roman Polanski.

OPPOSITE: Steve McQueen had a famous passion for motor racing, which he was to indulge with the making of the movie *Le Mans* (1971), which he part-financed. He is pictured on location during time trials for the Le Mans 24 hour race. Actual footage of the race was shown in the movie.

ABOVE: The Le Mans start line: in the 1971 race the traditional start, where the cars lined up against the pit wall in their qualifying order (shown here in a still from the movie), was abandoned for safety reasons and substituted with a rolling start, which has been in use ever since.

1971

ABOVE: Julie Christie (left) with Jane Birkin (center) and Gabrielle Crawford at Christie's home in 1971. That same year, Christie starred in *The Go-Between*, which won a Grand Prix at Cannes.

OPPOSITE: Director Alfred Hitchcock with actors Barry Foster and Bernard Cribbins, on location in London during the filming of *Frenzy*. Much of the shooting took place in and around London's Covent Garden market, where the director's father had worked as a market trader. Based upon Arthur La Bern's novel *Goodbye Piccadilly, Farewell Leicester Square*, *Frenzy* was Hitchcock's penultimate film, and was widely seen as a return to form after the political thrillers *Torn Curtain* and *Topaz*.

ABOVE: Oliver Reed's hard-drinking, hard-loving lifestyle made his real life something of a movie. His portrayal of the sexually ambiguous Gerald in the 1969 movie *Women in Love* was an earlier collaboration with director Ken Russell. Russell's controversial *The Devils*, showing explicit nudity and sexual ecstasy amongst nuns, was one of two movies featuring Reed in 1971. Oliver Reed's sexual magnetism was the perfect vehicle for new ideas about sexual freedom being portrayed in the media.

OPPOSITE: The Stonewall Riots in Greenwich Village in 1969 gave rise to an active Gay campaigning movement, the Gay Liberation Front, which published its newspaper *Gay* within six months of the riots and organized the first Gay Pride March on Gay Liberation Day the following year. The rebellion against repressive by-laws and statutes followed a similar formula around the world, taken up in London, Paris, Stockholm, and Berlin in 1971.

come together

NO 8   5p

SISTERS AND BROTHERS

COME OUT AND FIGHT AGAINST OPPRESSION

gay day and *demo*

SATURDAY AUGUST 28

SPEAKERS CORNER 1·30pm

Declaration of   Age of Consent

1972

Carroll O'Connor as Archie Bunker and Jean Stapleton his long-suffering and devoted wife, Edith, were the couple at the center of top CBS TV sitcom, *All in the Family*, which first aired in 1971 and ran for nine seasons. The show was based on the UK series *Till Death Us Do Part* and, like its British predecessor, allowed major issues of sexuality, racism, and women's liberation to be brought into the open for the first time in the world of American TV sitcom.

1972

OPPOSITE: Police officers at Wood Green Police Station, London, forced to work by candlelight due to the miners' strike that took place during January and February. The Central Electricity Generating Board introduced electricity-saving blackouts, which lasted up to nine hours a day in some areas. It was the first time that British miners had resorted to industrial action since 1926 and it led Prime Minister Edward Heath to declare a state of emergency.

RIGHT: Wives, sporting their husbands' helmets, marched on Parliament to protest on behalf of the miners.

1972

OPPOSITE: Members of US pop group The Osmonds, Alan, Donny, and "Little" Jimmy Osmond. In 1972 the Osmonds were to enjoy hits with "Down By the Lazy River," "Hold Her Tight," and "Crazy Horses," which narrowly missed the top of the UK charts. Meanwhile, Jimmy would reach the UK number one spot with his solo recording, "Long Haired Lover from Liverpool."

ABOVE: *Top of the Pops* was the weekly BBC TV pop music show, featuring songs and artists from the current chart. It ran from 1964 to 2006 with bands performing in front of a live studio audience with varied dancing ability. Jimmy Savile, pictured third from the right, presented the first show and co-hosted the final program, with countless performances in between. Savile's eccentric appearance, his strong northern accent, and distinctive patter combined with waving a trademark cigar endeared him to a wide audience. In 1972 *Top of the Pops* introduced new theme music which generated immediate audience recognition—a cover by session musicians of C.C.S.'s instrumental version of Led Zeppelin's "Whole Lotta Love."

1972

OPPOSITE: Raymond Burr plays wheelchair-bound Chief Detective Robert T. Ironside in the long running TV series *Ironside*, set in San Francisco's police department The show ran from September 1967 to February 1975—eight seasons and 199 episodes. Although highly successful as Ironside, Burr's previous incarnation as attorney Perry Mason was one of the most successful series of the 1960s, remembered with equal affection by Burr's many fans.

ABOVE: A still from the 1972 TV series *Colditz,* starring Robert Wagner and David McCallum. Factually based on the World War II high security prison for captured allied combatants, the show ran for two seasons, starting in October 1972. With strong characterization the series unusually set out to show the Colditz story from the

1972

OPPOSITE: British paratroopers run through the streets of Londonderry, Northern Ireland. Civil disturbances in Londonderry in 1972 brought British troops out onto the streets, culminating on January 30, 1972—"Bloody Sunday"—when 13 people were killed.

ABOVE: Troops and thousands of marchers proceed in silence in Dungiven after "Bloody Sunday." At first the soldiers barred the way with barbed wire, but after discussion allowed those bearing the white crosses (commemorating the dead) to place them on the steps of the Royal Ulster Constabulary barracks.

ABOVE: The Tutankhamun exhibition at the British Museum in 1972 was one of the most successful London had ever known, with long lines forming daily. Here the priceless gold mask of the young Egyptian king is unveiled for the first time. The 21in mask weighs 22.5 pounds and is inlaid with cornelian, turquoise, and lapis.

OPPOSITE: Hippies get back to nature at a summer rock festival.

1972

OPPOSITE: Central Park is one of New York City's greatest treasures occupying more than a square mile of precious Manhattan real estate. In the 1970s the Park became a hub of free expression, from informal gatherings, "Be-ins," and protests to nude sunbathing and pot-smoking. Giant free concerts in 1972 included Simon & Garfunkel. The Park's reputation for not being a safe place after dark was justified, but there were many more dangerous places in the City.

RIGHT: The North Tower of the World Trade Center was completed in 1972, becoming the world's tallest building at 1,368 feet until supplanted by the Sears Tower, Chicago, two years later. The building of the twin South Tower was completed in 1973. The WTC complex of seven buildings changed the Manhattan skyline forever, but its destruction in 2001 would make an even greater impact on New York City.

OPPOSITE: Actor Robert Wagner with his actress wife, Natalie Wood, and her daughter, Natasha. Having been married for five years, the couple divorced in 1962, with both going on to marry other people soon afterwards. Remarkably, however, Wagner and Wood remarried ten years later, in a ceremony held on board their yacht *Splendor*. Tragically, in 1981 Wood was to fall overboard from the same yacht and drown.

ABOVE: A scene from the comedy series *Are You Being Served?*, which first appeared on British screens as a pilot episode in 1972. Set in the clothing department of a large department store, the sitcom starred Frank Thornton, Mollie Sugden, John Inman, and Wendy Richard, and was highly successful, running for some 13 years and attracting audiences of up to 22 million viewers.

1972

ABOVE: *The Candidate*, directed by Michael Ritchie, takes the lid off the American election process and its politics. The central character, Bill McKay, played by Robert Redford, stands as a Democratic candidate to oppose a popular and well established California Republican. Marvin Lucas, played by Peter Boyle, is the election specialist running McKay's campaign. The screenplay, written by Jeremy Larner who was a speechwriter for Senator Eugene McCarthy, gained the Best Writing Oscar.

OPPOSITE: British Conservative Prime Minister Edward Heath. In January 1972 Heath signed a treaty admitting Britain into the Common Market. The new community of European countries would have a population bigger than that of the United States.

ABOVE: Marie Schneider in the movie *Last Tango in Paris,* which was released in October to a storm of controversy; the sexual drama was devised by writer and director Bernardo Bertolucci and based on a sexual fantasy about making love with a stranger.

OPPOSITE: The team from children's TV program *Magpie,* ITV's equivalent of *Blue Peter* in the 1970s. Douglas Rae, Sue Stranks, and Mick Robertson are decked out here in state-of-the-art fashion designed by Mr. Freedom.

1972

ABOVE AND OPPOSITE: The inimitable Mick Jagger, sex symbol and lead singer of the Rolling Stones, and Bianca De Macias, the striking model from Nicaragua whom Jagger married in May 1971. A few years later they were divorced, by which time Jagger faced a paternity suit from Marsha Hunt and had been cited in Marianne Faithfull's divorce proceedings. He finally took up with Bryan Ferry's Texan ex-girlfriend Jerry Hall, whom he married but divorced in 1999.

1972

ABOVE: US Olympic basketball players celebrate for a brief moment as they mistakenly rejoice over what they thought was a victory over the Soviet Union in the final game of the Olympic basketball tournament in Munich, September 9, 1972. With USA leading 50–49, officials reset the clock, giving the Soviet team another chance to score. They took it, bringing the score to 51–50 in favor of the Soviet Union, and their opponents protested the decision in vain.

OPPOSITE: British boxer John Conteh had a successful career in the light-heavyweight division; this culminated in 1974 when he became the first British fighter for 25 years to win the world crown by beating Argentinian Jorge Ahumada.

1972

OPPOSITE: The Vietnam War continues—sandbagged bunkers topped with canvas play home to the 4th Infantry Division at a forward camp near the Cambodian border

RIGHT: Edward, Duke of Windsor died on May 28, ending what many considered to be the romance of the century, after King Edward VIII abdicated the throne of Great Britain in 1936 in order to marry divorcee Wallis Simpson, pictured here with the Queen Mother. His funeral was held at St George's Chapel, Windsor Castle, on June 5.

1972

LEFT: The maxi skirt was as fashionable as the mini skirt in the early 1970s. The model is wearing a black velvet skirt, with tartan taffeta cummerbund and white crepe pintucked blouse.

OPPOSITE: Hot pants and platform shoes, all in silver and gold leather, were an alternative to the maxi skirt.

ABOVE: A member of the Palestinian terrorist group Black September, seen on the balcony of the Olympic Village during the Munich Summer Games. In the early hours of September 5, eight masked men attacked members of the Israeli team as they slept, killing wrestling coach Moshe Weinberg and weightlifter Yossef Romano, and taking nine others hostage.

OPPOSITE: An Israeli athlete weeps after the massacre at the Olympic Games in Munich. Tragically all nine of the Israeli hostages were killed, along with four of their Arab kidnappers and a German policeman, during a German police attempt to free the hostages at Fürstenfeldbruck airbase.

ABOVE: US swimmer Marc Spitz at the 1972 Summer Olympics, where he set a new world record by winning seven gold medals in a single Olympics. Incredibly, he also broke the world record time for each of the seven events in which he participated. In 1999 Spitz would be recognized as one of the five sportsmen of the century by the International Olympic Committee, and his record stood until 2008, when American swimmer Michael Phelps won eight gold medals at the Beijing Summer Olympics.

OPPOSITE: Mary Peters, seen competing in the long jump on her way to winning gold in the pentathlon at the Olympic Games in Munich. Born in Lancashire, but raised in Belfast, Peters is credited with briefly bridging the sectarian divide in Northern Ireland as her battle against the German favorite, Heide Rosendahl, captivated the public attention.

1972

OPPOSITE: The cast of the West End production of the musical *Godspell*, pictured during rehearsals for a television version. Largely based on the New Testament Gospel according to Matthew, the cast included David Essex as Jesus, and Jeremy Irons in the twin roles of John the Baptist and Judas Iscariot. The production provided both Essex and Irons with their first major acting roles.

ABOVE: *Carry on Matron*: Hattie Jacques (Matron) and Charles Hawtrey (Dr. Francis Goode) in a scene from the 26th in the popular *Carry On* movie series, of which 29 were made between 1958 and 1978 at Pinewood Studios near London. Like the others in the series, the movie was a mixture of satire, innuendo, and farce. The cast was composed of well-loved British character actors, many of whom also enjoyed long-running TV and stage careers.

ABOVE: Serial killer John Wayne Gacy pictured at his wedding to his second wife, Carole Hoff, in June 1972. Gacy spent many years picking up teenage runaways or male prostitutes. He would sexually abuse them before murdering them. In 1978, following an investigation, police discovered human bones beneath his house. After confessing to around 30 murders, Gacy spent 14 years on death row and died by lethal injection in 1994.

OPPOSITE: On July 21—"Bloody Friday"—22 IRA bombs exploded around Belfast, killing nine people and injuring 130. Two of the dead were soldiers, the rest were all civilians. British troops faced daily violence in the worst year of "the Troubles"; in this photograph soldiers are hit with petrol bombs on the streets of Belfast.

1972

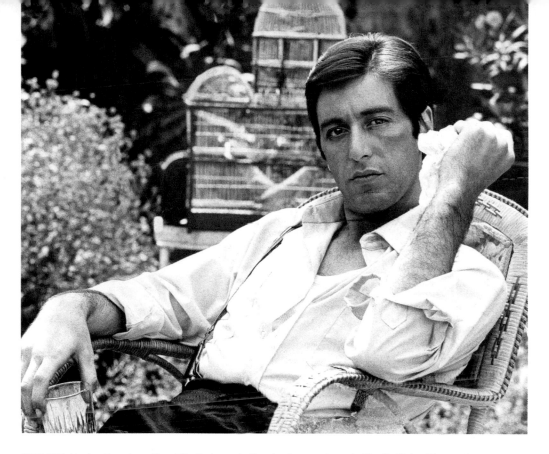

OPPOSITE: Marlon Brando as Don Vito Corleone in the classic gangster epic *The Godfather*. The movie was nominated for 11 Academy Awards, and won three: Best Picture, Best Adapted Screenplay, and Best Actor (for Brando) and has been ranked as the second best American film of all time by the American Film Institute.

ABOVE: When Francis Ford Coppola secured Al Pacino for the role of Michael Corleone in 1972's *The Godfather*, Pacino had made just two films, neither of which had brought him much attention. *The Godfather* and its sequel two years later did, however, and his performances made him much in demand in Hollywood. Between the two, he made *Serpico*, the true story of a New York cop out to expose police corruption (1973). It was shot by Sidney Lumet, with whom Pacino would work again on *Dog Day Afternoon* (1975), both films earning him further praise, and bringing his total Oscar nominations to four in four years.

OPPOSITE: Jack Nicklaus tees off at the British Open; although he lost here to Lee Trevino by a single shot, 1972 was a great year for Nicklaus, who won two majors—the Masters and the US Open.

ABOVE: Celebrity footballers Elton John and Rod Stewart train with Watford Football Club. Elton John would later be director and chairman of the club. Eventually, as principle investor, he owned it and, although no longer a majority shareholder today, he continues to support the club financially. 1972 saw the end of a period of success for Watford when the team was relegated to the Third Divison.

1973

The Miami Dolphins won Super Bowl VIII in 1973 following their perfect 1972 season. They were only the fourth NFL team to have a perfect season and the first in its history to appear at the Super Bowl three years in a row. The Dolphins were coached for 25 years by the legendary Don Shula, the most successful chief coach in the game. Wearing the 59 jersey is Doug Swift; Bob Heinz is the number 72.

1973

LEFT: Steve McQueen plays tortured French prisoner Papillon in the movie of the same name; the distinctive butterfly tattoo on his chest earns him the nickname. The movie is based on a fictionalized account of Henri Charriere's wrongful imprisonment in French penal colonies in the Caribbean and his efforts to escape and to be avenged.

OPPOSITE: Less rugged-looking, Cyril Smith, the 27-stone Liberal member of parliament for Rochdale, attempts to knit in a charity "Knational Knit In" for arthritis and rheumatism. Well-known for his humor and appetite, Mr. Smith was not, however, skilled on the domestic front.

1973

OPPOSITE: Bobby Moore (right) and Sir Alf Ramsey, captain and manager of the England football team in the 1966 and 1970 World Cup tournaments. Bobby Moore played for England from 1962 to 1973, leading them to victory against West Germany in 1966. Moore saved some of his finest performances for the 1970 World Cup in Mexico, when he was particularly outstanding in the match against Brazil. Controversy preceded the tournament when Moore was accused of stealing a gold bracelet, a charge on which he was later found innocent. Sir Alf continued to manage England until 1974.

ABOVE: The 1970s witnessed the "streaker" phenomenon—characters who shed their clothes and "streaked" in front of others in public places, sometimes just for dramatic effect, sometimes to make some kind of statement. Here a streaker takes off on a film set in London.

1973

OPPOSITE: Marc Bolan, who, with his band T-Rex, was part of the "glam rock" movement of the early 1970s. In 1971 and 1972, T-Rex were the best-selling singles band, with hits such as "Metal Guru," "Ride a White Swan," and "Get it on." Significantly, one of his concert tours in 1976 marked the change of times in the decade when he was supported by punk band The Damned. Bolan was tragically killed when his car crashed into a tree at high speed in September 1977.

ABOVE: *The Way We Were*. Barbra Streisand and Robert Redford co-starred in this Sydney Pollack movie released in October 1973. Based on a screenplay by Arthur Laurents and touching on big political and social issues, Pollack's handling of the story made it the romantic movie of the decade, with McCarthyism more of a sub-plot. The movie was a major success, adding luster to the film careers of both actors, earning two Oscars and a further four nominations; the soundtrack, released by Sony and including the title song sung by Streisand, reached 20 in the *Billboard* 200 chart.

ABOVE: John Spencer, along with Ray Reardon and Alex Higgins, put snooker on the map and dominated the up-and- coming sport throughout the 1970s. In the 1973 World Snooker Championship, the match of the competition was the semi-final between Spencer and Reardon. Reardon won 23–22. Spencer had to settle for winning the Norwich Union Open.

OPPOSITE: Jockey Ron Turcotte sits atop of Secretariat racing in the lead at the Preakness Stakes at Pimlico Race Track, Baltimore, Maryland. This was the second leg of the Triple Crown, one of the USA's most prestigious competitions, which Secretariat won by the largest margin of victory in the history of the Stakes.

1973

LEFT: Rock star David Bowie, seen here in his Ziggy Stardust guise. Flame-red hair, vivid makeup, shimmering skintight Lurex suits on a razor-thin body, and platform boots were some of the hallmarks of his style.

OPPOSITE: Guitarist Jeff Beck with his girlfriend, the fashion model Celia Hammond. Having made her name with *Vogue* magazine during the 1960s, later in her career Hammond would find fame as an anti-fur campaigner. Meanwhile, in 1973 Beck had dissolved the Jeff Beck Group and would tour the UK, the US, and Japan as part of Beck, Bogert, and Appice, with bassist Tim Bogert and drummer Carmine Appice, both formerly of Vanilla Fudge.

1973

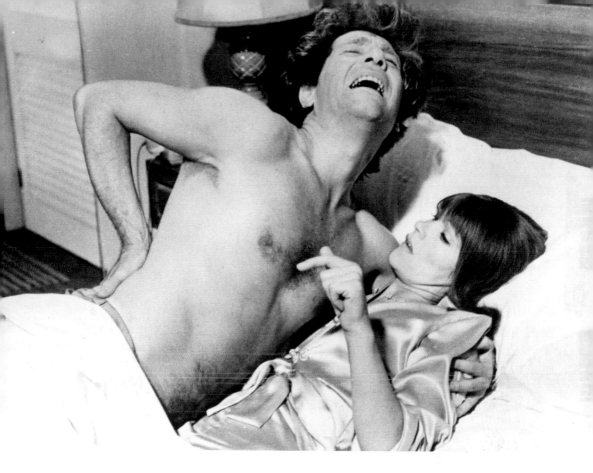

OPPOSITE: Her Royal Highness Princess Anne with Mark Phillips at Buckingham Palace on the return from their wedding on November 14, 1973. As the bride and groom were world-class horse riders there were many sporting friends among the 1,500 guests at Westminster Abbey. Princess Anne had won a European gold medal while Mark Phillips had an Olympic gold.

ABOVE: George Segal and Glenda Jackson in the comedy film *A Touch of Class,* which is about a happily married American man who embarks upon a love affair with a divorcee he meets in London. Glenda Jackson's performance as Vicki Allessio would earn her the Academy Award for Best Actress, while the film was nominated for a further four Oscars, including Best Picture.

ABOVE: Kevin Keegan, leading light for Liverpool Football Club in the 1970s, races to win the ball from Ken Burns of Birmingham in 1973, at the height of Liverpool's fortunes. Keegan appeared 230 times for Liverpool and scored 68 goals.

OPPOSITE: Jackie Stewart, champion Formula One racing driver, celebrates winning the German Grand Prix in 1973. His five victories that year gave him his third Drivers' Championship. It proved to be Stewart's last season in Formula One as a driver.

1973

LEFT: Entertainer and game-show host Bruce Forsyth with his girlfriend, Anthea Redfern. Having met at a "Miss Lovely Legs" competition, the couple embarked upon an affair, with Redfern going on to join Forsyth as his assistant on the BBC TV show *The Generation Game*.

OPPOSITE: The popular TV Western *Alias Smith & Jones* was inspired by the movie *Butch Cassidy and The Sundance Kid* and originally featured Ben Murphy (right) and Pete Duel. When Duel killed himself in 1971, Roger Davis stepped into the role of Hannibal Heyes for the last 17 episodes.

1973

LEFT: In 1973, the same year that she graduated from St. Thomas Aquinas High School in Fort Lauderdale, Florida, Chris Evert reached the finals of both the French Open and Wimbledon, coming second to Australian Margaret Court and fellow American Billie Jean King respectively. From August of that year however, Evert would win 125 consecutive matches on clay, losing just seven sets—a record that remains unbroken to this day.

OPPOSITE: Romanian tennis star Ilie Nastase pictured in a dispute with the umpire at Wimbledon in 1973. By the end of the year Nastase was world number one, having won some 17 tournaments, including the French Open, which he clinched without dropping a set, a third consecutive Masters Cup, and the men's doubles title at Wimbledon with partner Jimmy Connors.

1973

ABOVE: Led Zeppelin's ninth US tour in summer 1973 set new box office records, grossing over $4m from 36 shows, including performing to 56,800 fans at Tampa Stadium, Florida, which broke the Beatles' record set at Shea Stadium, NY, in 1965. Instead of the traditional tour bus they hired a converted passenger jet named *Starship*, equipped with all the comforts needed for Zeppelin's rock lifestyle. The 1973 tour was filmed and released in 1976 as a feature film, *The Song Remains the Same*. Included in this was the theft of their takings from three nights at Madison Square Garden from the safe deposit box of their hotel, the Drake, a loss of over $200,000.

OPPOSITE: American pop singer Diana Ross left the Supremes at the start of the decade. Her solo career took off rapidly and was boosted by an Academy nomination for Best Actress for her role as Billie Holiday in 1972 movie *Lady Sings the Blues*.

1973

OPPOSITE: Running back O.J. Simpson of the Buffalo Bills avoids the tackle attempt by an unidentified New York Jets player during a game on December 16, 1973, at Shea Stadium. Simpson established a new single season record for yards gained, with a total of 2,003 yards. Simpson later moved into acting and achieved considerable notoriety in the 1990s when implicated in the murder of his estranged wife.

RIGHT: Heavyweight boxer George Foreman. On January 22, 1973, Foreman stunned the boxing world by defeating the previously unbeaten, undisputed world champion, "Smokin" Joe Frazier, who hit the canvas six times before the referee stopped the fight in the second round. The contest took place in Jamaica, and was billed as "The Sunshine Showdown."

ABOVE: A scene of famine in Senegal. In 1973 a drought that had effectively begun in 1969 reached its peak, affecting a vast band of territory across Africa, from Senegal to Somalia, and threatening the lives of millions of people. Parts of both East and West Africa were severely affected, with hundreds of thousands of people in countries such as Senegal and Ethiopia being displaced as they migrated into neighboring regions in an attempt to avoid starvation.

OPPOSITE: Publishing tycoon and former member of parliament Robert Maxwell pictured in his study following a meeting of Pergamon Press shareholders. In 1973 the Department of Trade and Industry published a highly critical report into Maxwell's management of the business, which not only suggested that he had released misleading information regarding the company's finances, but concluded that he was essentially unfit to control a public company.

ABOVE: Actors Rodney Bewes (left) and James Bolam as Bob and Terry in the highly popular British sitcom *Whatever Happened to the Likely Lads?*, which was written by Dick Clement and Ian La Frenais.

OPPOSITE: Peter Falk starred as Police Lt. Columbo in the NBC TV series *Columbo* which ran from 1968 to 2003, a total of 69 episodes. Falk supplied his own characteristic wardrobe and his distinctive creased raincoat was complemented by a chewed-on cigar and a distracted manner, aided and abetted by his glass eye. The show attracted many notable guest stars and Steven Spielberg was a guest director in the first run of the show. Falk also won an Emmy in the first season of 1971.

1973

ABOVE: A victim of the IRA car bomb attack, which took place outside the Central Criminal Court in Old Bailey, London, in March, the same day as a referendum in Northern Ireland about the region remaining part of the UK. Following a breakdown in talks between the IRA and the British government in 1972, the IRA took its bombing campaign to the British mainland in early 1973. Four car bombs were planted in London, and although the IRA team was betrayed to the police by an informer, two of the devices exploded, killing one and injuring 180 others.

OPPOSITE: A second bomb exploded outside the Metropolitan Police headquarters in Great Scotland Yard, Whitehall. The attacks were carried out by 11 members of the "Belfast Brigade," who had hijacked the cars used in the bombings in Northern Ireland, before driving them to London. The team attempted to escape by plane, but ten members, including Gerry Kelly, Hugh Feeney, and sisters Dolours and Marian Price, were arrested at Heathrow Airport.

Lyricist Tim Rice and composer Andrew Lloyd Webber. Initially released as a concept album before being staged as a play in the West End and on Broadway, in 1973 the duo's rock opera *Jesus Christ Superstar* was released as a movie, and became one of the highest-grossing films of the year. Its two principal stars, Ted Neely and Carl Anderson, who played Jesus and Judas respectively, would both later be nominated for Golden Globe Awards for their performances.

Michael Crawford and Michelle Dotrice pictured in an episode of the British situation comedy *Some Mothers Do 'Ave 'Em*, in which Crawford was cast as the well-meaning, but incredibly accident prone Frank Spencer. The show ran for two series in 1973, returning for two Christmas specials in 1974 and 1975, with a third series being broadcast in 1978. The show became famous for its slapstick humor, with Crawford performing some of the most dangerous stunts seen in British comedy. In the 1980s Crawford took the male lead in Andrew Lloyd Webber's musical spectacular *Phantom of the Opera*.

1973

ABOVE: At the Watergate hearings Jeb Stuart Magruder is sworn in by Senator Sam Ervin, Democratic National Committee chairman, at the beginning of his testimony before the Senate Watergate Committee in Washington, DC, June 14, 1973. Magruder, a former top aide to President Nixon, was the only witness to contend that President Nixon (pictured opposite) ordered the break-in that ultimately led to his resignation. Magruder served a jail sentence of seven months for his role in the Watergate scandal.

ABOVE: The scaling down of US military action and resources in Vietnam in 1973 encouraged the Vietcong to recover lost territory. Sentry geese help guard the strategic Y-Bridge in Saigon. The geese acted as an early warning system for the US troops guarding the bridge, which was Saigon's main highway link to the South.

OPPOSITE: A South Vietnamese paratrooper wounded by a shelling attack on his unit southwest of Quang Tri waits for medics to give him an injection.

ABOVE: At the British Footwear Show in 1973 platform heels were all the rage, coming in all colors, shapes, and sizes. Heel heights ranged from 2 to 5 inches, and platform heights from half an inch to 4 inches.

OPPOSITE: A girl pictured wearing a halter-neck top and maxi skirt, both of which were highly popular during the early 1970s. The halter neckline was employed in a huge range of clothing, including swimwear, evening gowns, catsuits, and maxi dresses with cutaway armholes. Inspired by the long, flowing ethnic skirts favored by hippies during the late 1960s, the ankle-length maxi skirt hit the Parisian catwalks in 1970, and was soon to be found in boutiques all over the world.

1973

ABOVE: Leeds United goalkeeper David Harvey, full back Paul Reaney and captain Billy Bremner prepare to defend a goal-bound shot delivered by Southampton's Wayne Talkes. Under the management of Don Revie, who would subsequently take charge of the England team, Leeds began the 1973–74 season with a record 29 games unbeaten, and would go on to take victory in the First Division.

OPPOSITE: Bob Stokoe, the delighted manager of Sunderland Football Club, embraces his player Ian Porterfield, scorer of the winning goal against Leeds in the 1973 FA Cup Final. Stokoe was not known for such public displays of affection.

1973

ABOVE: Actor and director Lord Laurence Olivier and the English theater director Peter Hall on the terrace of the National Theatre, London. Modernist architect Denys Lasdun freely admitted he knew nothing of designing theaters to the committee appointing him but promised to learn. Made of concrete inside and out, it is seen by some as a fine example of 1970s brutalist architecture and by others as a blot on the landscape of London.

OPPOSITE: Controversial pop idol Vincent Damon Furnier, better known as Alice Cooper, photographed in his stage makeup. Pioneer of heavy metal, and proponent of extreme stage performance, including decapitating dolls and a guillotine with executioner, eponymous band Alice Cooper released two albums in 1973: their most commercially successful *Billion Dollar Babies* in February and then *Muscle of Love* at the end of the year.

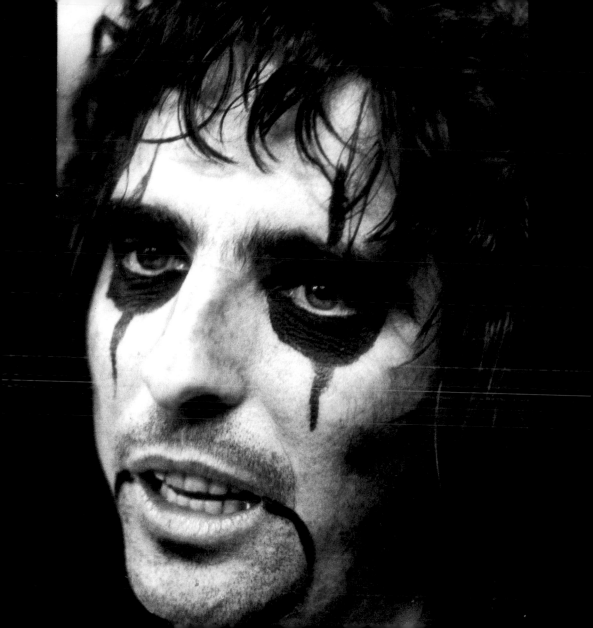

ABOVE: Israeli troops set Damascus in their sights during the Yom Kippur War. Egypt and Syria coordinated their attack on Israel on October 6—the most holy day of the Jewish calendar. After initial successes aided by the element of surprise, the Arab attackers were pushed back on Mt. Hermon on the Golan Heights and outflanked in Egypt. On each front, Israeli troops came within tactical range of Cairo and Damascus respectively. The war ended on October 26 and was followed soon after by the Camp David Accords, which improved relations between Egypt and Israel, Egypt becoming the first Arab nation to recognize the State of Israel.

OPPOSITE: An Arab family from the Syrian town of Jabta al Chatab wave a white flag to the Israelis. Much of the town evacuated along with the Syrian army in the wake of the Israeli advance.

Houston, Texas: On September 20, 1973, 55-year-old Bobby Riggs played 29-year-old Billie Jean King in a televised game of tennis that commentators dubbed "The Battle of the Sexes." King easily won the match 6–4, 6–3, 6–3, thus disproving Riggs' assertion that women's tennis was so inferior that a top woman player would be unable to beat him, even when given an advantage because of a substantial age difference.

161

1974

Muhammad Ali fought twice in 1974—
against Joe Frazier at the beginning of
the year and against George Foreman in
Kinshasa in October, a contest that was
dubbed "the rumble in the jungle." Ali
defeated Frazier in 12 rounds, but his bid
to regain the World Heavyweight title by
defeating the holder George Foreman was
a more dramatic event (right). Ali soaked
up all that Foreman could throw at him,
waiting until Foreman tired before moving
forward to attack. A straight right to the
chin in round eight felled Foreman and Ali
regained the world title.

1974

LEFT: The mid-1970s look from the Parisian flea market—chunky cardigan, long knitted scarf, and baggy pants.

OPPOSITE: A more prosaic look on the streets of London. The midi skirt came in, with stripes for spring, and the inevitable platform soles.

1974

ABOVE: The fresh-faced David Cassidy, star of TV's *The Partridge Family* and singer of other artists' songs, reduced thousands of screaming teens to complete hysteria. One hit followed another—"I Think I Love You" and "How Can I Be Sure" were but two and the fans couldn't get enough of him. David soon tired of being mobbed and employed strong-arm men to protect him on his public appearances.

OPPOSITE: Elton John in one of his Crocodile Rock-style performances. Composer of some of the 1970s' best melodies, including "Your Song," "Candle in the Wind," "Daniel," and "Goodbye Yellow Brick Road," Elton John achieved enormous international fame which was to continue for three decades. Throughout the 1970s he was never out of the US album charts, and in 1974 tickets for his three Los Angeles shows were sold out in minutes.

ABOVE: US President Richard Nixon pictured with Russian Communist Party leader Leonid Brezhnev in Moscow. With the end of US involvement in Vietnam the previous year, relations between America and the USSR were improving. Back home, however, Nixon was facing impeachment over the Watergate scandal and on August 9 he became the first US president to resign from office. As a result, his Vice-President Gerald Ford was sworn in as the 38th President of the United States that same day.

OPPOSITE: Leaders of the three main UK political parties of the 1970s caught in a rare moment of unity, as they each place £1.00 in a silver rose-bowl for charity. From left to right: Edward Heath (Conservative), Jeremy Thorpe (Liberal), and Harold Wilson (Labour). Wilson preceded Heath as Prime Minister and also followed him into office after a general election in February 1974.

ABOVE: Some of the cast of the long-running series *Upstairs Downstairs*, which told the story of the Bellamy family and their servants, beginning in 1903 and ending in 1930. The series, written by Eileen Atkins and Jean March (who played Rose, pictured on the extreme right), won numerous awards on both sides of the Atlantic.

OPPOSITE: The Goodies were Bill Oddie, Graeme Garden, and Tim Brooke-Taylor, pictured here (left to right) on their trademark mode of transport—the trandem. Their offbeat TV series *The Goodies* was a mixture of zany sketches and situation comedy but as the name implies there was perhaps more of a message in their humor than their Monty Python contemporaries. Like the Pythons, the Goodies were graduates of the Cambridge Footlights school of comedy. The show ran from 1970 to 1982 broadcasting 70 episodes.

1974

ABOVE: Bill Shankly, manager of Liverpool football team, after his farewell match. Shankly was Liverpool's much-loved manager for 15 years from 1959 to 1974, during which time he brought the team up from the lower half of the Second Division to heights of glory in the First Division. A statue to Shankly, with arms outstretched in the pose of the above photograph, stands proudly in front of Anfield's Kop end, reminding fans of his achievements at the club and the foundations he laid for future success.

OPPOSITE: Hank Aaron, number 44, of the Atlanta Braves hits his 715th career home run, breaking Babe Ruth's long-standing record, at Atlanta-Fulton County Stadium on April 8, 1974, in Atlanta, Georgia.

1974

OPPOSITE: Swedish pop stars Abba, winners of the 1974 Eurovision Song Contest with the song "Waterloo." The contest, and the subsequent release of "Waterloo" as a single, brought ABBA international recognition, with the song reaching the US top ten, and the top of the charts in the UK, South Africa, and throughout much of Europe. In the wake of their newfound success, the group would embark upon a European tour later in the year.

ABOVE: Star of TV detective-drama *Kojak*, Telly Savalas, meets the Queen at the Royal Variety Performance at the London Palladium. The Queen had a soft spot for the TV show and on a later visit to Washington, Savalas would be invited to a reception honoring Her Majesty at the White House.

1974

ABOVE: On October 5, 1974, the Provisional IRA detonated two six pound bombs in two separate public houses in Guildford, Surrey, which were known to be frequented by British servicemen and women. Five people were killed and numerous others were seriously injured at the Horse and Groom (pictured), although no one was seriously hurt at the nearby Seven Stars, which was evacuated after the first blast. Eleven people were convicted in the aftermath of the bombings, all of whom would later be exonerated of any involvement, having served up to 15 years in prison. The story of one of the 11 was made into the 1993 movie *In the Name of the Father.*

OPPOSITE: The US may have been winding down its presence in Vietnam but the losses continued up to the final evacuation of Saigon in 1975. Here Battalion Commander Lt. Colonel Ardie E. McClure of the 1st Battalion 8th Cavalry Regiment calls for assistance as he evacuates Private First Class Lyle, who was wounded in fighting near Bong Son.

1974

OPPOSITE: The Ideal Home Exhibition was held every year in London to display the latest in lifestyle developments; here we see a dramatic and luxurious fireplace and boldly printed wallpaper in the lounge of the "Mowbray House" by Yorkshire Homes. Although space-age styling, bold patterns, and eclecticism remained a feature of interior design during the 1970s, after the affluence and innovation of the 1960s many people turned to companies such as Schreiber to furnish their homes inexpensively.

ABOVE: A woman pictured cooking in a kitchen on show at the Ideal Home Exhibition. Innovations in the kitchen during the 1970s included food processors such as the Magimix, and later the microwave oven, but for many it was the freezer that first revolutionized domestic eating habits, with one in ten British households owning a freezer by 1974, and specialist frozen food outlets opening on the high street.

ABOVE: Brian Clough receives a standing ovation from football fans as he makes his managerial debut of Leeds United at Elland Road, despite having not only criticized former manager Don Revie, but also the Leeds United team for their aggressive playing style. Just 44 days later, however, Clough was sacked by the board of directors, having led the club to one of its worst ever starts to a season, and after reported clashes with senior players Billy Bremner, Norman Hunter, and Johnny Giles.

OPPOSITE: Liverpool's Kevin Keegan involved in a fight with Leeds United's Billy Bremner during the 1974 FA Charity Shield game at Wembley. In a match characterized by aggressive play, both Keegan and Bremner were sent off after trading blows. They were each fined £500 and banned for the next 11 matches. It was the first Charity Shield match ever to be televised, and the last time that Liverpool manager Bill Shankly would lead his team onto the pitch.

1974

President Gerald Ford (left) is sworn in as the 38th President of the United States next to his wife Betty and Chief of Justice Warren Burger in Washington, DC. Ford sought to heal America after the trauma of the Watergate scandal that forced Richard Nixon from office in 1974.

1974

ABOVE: Neil Diamond had his first major success in 1969 with "Sweet Caroline," which was followed by classics such "I am, I said" and the 1979 hit "Forever in Blue Jeans." He and Barbra Streisand had a number one hit in 1978 with his own composition "You Don't Bring Me Flowers."

OPPOSITE: American singer Stevie Wonder feeding the pigeons in Trafalgar Square during his visit to London. After overcoming a life-threatening auto accident in 1973, which left him in a coma, 1974 was to be a high point in Wonder's career when for the second year in a row he was awarded five Grammys, including Album of the Year. For UK fans Wonder's Rainbow Theatre concerts became a legend, while in the US his March concert at Madison Square Garden was a celebrated return to the stage.

ABOVE: Cast members from the US television program *The Waltons*, which starred Ralph Waite as John Walton, Richard Thomas as John Boy, and Michael Learned as Olivia Walton. In 1974 Learned's portrayal of the softly spoken Olivia would earn her a second consecutive Emmy for Lead Actress in a Drama Series.

OPPOSITE: Children at play in the alleyways between houses in Salford, near Manchester. A major feature of British industrial towns and cities, a great deal of back-to-back housing was demolished during the slum clearances of the 1960s and by the 1970s most had been removed to make way for new concrete housing estates and high-rises provided by local government.

1974

ABOVE: Ethiopian troops occupy the National Palace days after the overthrow of Emperor Haile Selassie in September 1974. Along with his cabinet members and the Patriarch of the Ethiopian Orthodox Church he was later executed by the Derg—the Russian-backed military committee which took over government in Ethiopia.

OPPOSITE: In 1974 heiress Patty Hearst was abducted from her apartment by members of guerilla group the Symbionese Liberation Army. Hearst was later pictured participating in a hold-up of the Hibernia Bank in San Francisco. Shortly after, she was arrested, and during her trial her defense strongly argued that she had been brainwashed by the guerilla group during her abduction. In 1976 Hearst was convicted and sentenced to 35 years' imprisonment, a term that was later commuted by President Jimmy Carter.

ABOVE: The Carpenters—sister and brother Karen (vocals and drums) and Richard (piano and vocals)—together the highly successful American pop duo took on a busy touring schedule in 1974, playing over 200 concerts around the world. They were so busy that this was the first year since their career took off when they didn't record an album. Their melodic, heavily orchestrated music and distinctive vocals were for many the sound of the 1970s. Karen died in 1983 aged only 33, from cardiac arrest arising from her eating disorder.

OPPOSITE: Set in smalltown America from the mid 1950s to the mid 1960s, ABC's *Happy Days* spawned one of sitcom's most famous characters, the Fonz, played by Henry Winkler (right). Rock musician Suzi Quatro (center) makes an appearance in this episode, playing a character called Leather Tuscadero.

1974

ABOVE: In 1974 British aristocrat Lord Lucan (pictured here aboard a yacht) was alleged to have murdered the family's nanny, Sandra Rivett. On the night of the murder Lucan disappeared and in a statement Lady Lucan named her husband as the killer. A year later, a jury agreed, but to this day there has been no verified sighting of the earl. In 1999 he was declared legally dead.

OPPOSITE: Greek Cypriot demonstrators march to protest against the Turkish invasion of Cyprus in July 1974.

1974

OPPOSITE: Lee Majors plays Steve Austin in *The Six Million Dollar Man*, the popular 1970s TV series. A former astronaut surviving devastating injuries, Austin is re-engineered to become a bionic superhero. The show achieved cult status with five seasons starting in 1974. One hundred episodes were recorded as well as six TV movies. Unsurprisingly the success of the show led to the *Bionic Woman* series, which starred Lindsy Wagner. Majors married *Charlie's Angels* star Farrah Fawcett in 1973 but they split in 1979.

ABOVE: Mia Farrow and Robert Redford star in *The Great Gatsby*, the 1974 movie based on F. Scott Fitzgerald's novel. It was directed by Jack Clayton with screenplay by Francis Ford Coppola, who was writing it while filming *The Godfather*. The movie won two Oscars, for Best Costume Design and Best Music. Mia Farrow was pregnant during shooting; she wore loose clothing and the camera kept tight to her upper half. Seen here is a young Patsy Kensit in the role of Pammy Buchanan.

ABOVE: Burt Reynolds played the pool-shooting, card-playing private detective opposite Dyan Cannon in the movie *Shamus*, which was a blend of action and comedy. From 1973 to 1980, Reynolds was a permanent fixture in the list of top ten box office attractions. The formula for his 1974 movie *The Longest Yard,* filmed in the Georgia State Prison, was so successful that he would appear in the remake in 2005.

OPPOSITE: Michael Caine and Glenda Jackson toast each other at the British Film Awards in 1974. Caine won Best Actor for his role in *Sleuth*, while Jackson won Best Actress for *A Touch of Class.*

Actresses Julie Christie and Goldie Hawn in the movie *Shampoo,* produced and co-written by Warren Beatty and in which he also starred. The film's timeline coincides with the election of Richard Nixon and it was released at the height of the Watergate scandal, but its main theme is sexual politics. Despite its sharp satire, amusing plot, and star cast, the movie had stiff compeition in the Academy Awards, winning only one—Best Actress in a Supporting Role—but with three further nominations. It was a box office success, however, and remains a comedy classic.

1975

ABOVE: Gravel-voiced Rod Stewart was as famous for his range of blondes as for his hit records. Here he is seen with girlfriend and actress Britt Ekland in 1975, shortly after they met at a Los Angeles party. She was later to become his wife.

OPPOSITE: Mick Jagger's irresistible stage presence. The "Stones Tour of the Americas '75" put on 46 shows during June and August. The tour was famously announced in May to the waiting US fans, not by traditional press conference but by the band performing "Brown Sugar" on the back of a truck moving slowly down Broadway in New York. This was Ronnie Wood's debut tour with the band, though he was not officially named as a Rolling Stone until December. Billy Preston played keyboards.

1975

ABOVE: Chaotic scenes on the roof of the American Embassy where evacuees try to board the last flight out of Saigon, April 30, 1975. A plainclothes American punches a Vietnamese man as he tries to climb into the helicopter.

OPPOSITE: A mob of terrified Vietnamese people scale the wall of the US Embassy in Saigon, fleeing the advancing Vietcong and trying to get to the helicopter pickup zone on April 29, 1975.

OPPOSITE: Freddie Mercury, flamboyant stage performer and extraordinary musician, was front man for rock band Queen. In 1975 their album *A Night at the Opera*, reputedly the most expensive album ever made, rocked the world, especially its chart-topping single "Bohemian Rhapsody," which was accompanied by one of the most famous music videos of all time. Mercury's early death at 46 from an AIDS-related condition left a colorful gap in rock music, but a great legacy of hits and memorable performances

ABOVE: David Bowie, rock idol of the 1970s, rides into town. In 1975 Bowie went in a completely different direction when he filmed *The Man Who Fell to Earth* at Knebworth Park, near London. By 1976 he had moved to Berlin, where he wrote *Heroes*, and became a near-recluse.

1975

LEFT: The first black American to be selected to play in the US Davis Cup team, Arthur Ashe won four Grand Slam titles, beginning with the US Open in 1968 and ending with Wimbledon in 1975. Ashe's contribution to sport and society was honored by the creation of the Arthur Ashe Stadium at Flushing Meadow, New York, which was opened in 1997.

OPPOSITE: Alan Taylor scores the second of his two goals for West Ham in their 2–0 victory against Fulham in the FA Cup final.

ABOVE: *Tiswas* is generally understood to be the acronym for *Today Is Saturday Watch And Smile*: pictured here are Chris Tarrant and Sally James, co-presenters of this 1970s cult children's TV program that was watched by as many adults as children on a Saturday morning. The show launched the career of Chris Tarrant and developed the profile of Lenny Henry, who made regular appearances. Its anarchic style was spread over eight series and 302 episodes, finally coming to an end in 1982.

OPPOSITE: The mid-1970s "page boy" hairstyle was a rediscovery of the 1950s style made popular by glamour model Betty Page. It was a style that could be adopted by either sex. In the changing sexual climate of the 1970s, unisex style was a popular development.

Four-times Indy 500 winner,
legendary US racing champion
A.J. Hoyt sits with the back
markers in this stretch of the
race; 1975 saw him win the
USAC Championship Car
Season—just one step in his
long and illustrious race career,
which made him the only
driver in history to have won
Indianapolis 500, Daytona 500,
24 Hours of Daytona, and 24
Hours of Le Mans.

OPPOSITE: Roger Daltrey, lead singer of rock group The Who, pictured live on stage. After the massive success of the LPs *Who's Next* and *Quadrophenia*, in 1975 the group released *The Who By Numbers*. It would reach the top ten on both sides of the Atlantic, but was much darker and more introspective than previous offerings. At the same time Ken Russell's film adaptation of the band's 1969 rock opera *Tommy* was released to critical acclaim, earning guitarist Pete Townshend an Oscar nomination for his musical score.

ABOVE: Graffiti protesting the innocence of convicted bank robber George Davis is daubed on a wall outside Headingly cricket ground, Leeds, where his supporters sabotaged the third Test match, England versus Australia, by digging up the pitch. Davis, having been imprisoned in 1975 for armed robbery, was released in 1976 by the Home Secretary Roy Jenkins, although he was later convicted of two further armed robberies.

OPPOSITE: Romanian gymnast Nadia Comaneci. Aged just 13, Comaneci secured her first major international titles in 1975, winning almost every event at the European Championships in Norway and collecting numerous medals at events in Romania and Canada. The following year she would win the all-around title at the Montreal Summer Olympics, scoring seven perfect tens along the way.

ABOVE: John Huston's 1975 movie *The Man Who Would Be King* was based on a Rudyard Kipling story set at the height of Britain's colonial empire and in the tradition of a 19th century epic drama. After considering a number of swashbuckling box office giants for the lead roles, at Paul Newman's suggestion Huston, pictured here on location, chose Sean Connery and Michael Caine.

1975

POLLING STATION

OPPOSITE: Margaret Thatcher, MP for Finchley, soon to become leader of the Conservative Party, arrives at the polling station to cast her vote. Labour Prime Minister Harold Wilson promised in his 1974 manifesto that the British electorate would have the chance to vote in a referendum on whether to remain in the European Economic Community, which the UK joined in 1973 under Edward Heath's Conservative government. The Labour rank and file were generally against membership, but the country's vote was 2–1 in favor of staying in the Common Market.

ABOVE: Margaret Thatcher pictured with her husband Denis decorating their new apartment in Scotney Castle, near Lamberhurst, Kent.

1975

OPPOSITE: Heartland rock singer and songwriter Bruce Springsteen in 1975, the breakout year for Springsteen. Already a seasoned circuit performer and having signed with his backing E Street Band to Columbia Records in 1972, a five night series at New York's Bottom Line Club that received major media attention finally got his show on the road. In October Springsteen made it onto the front covers of both *Time* and *Newsweek* in the same week and later in the year the Born to Run tour went to Europe, playing gigs in London, Stockholm, and Amsterdam.

ABOVE: Actress Elizabeth Taylor arriving at the Dorchester Hotel, London, with her husband Richard Burton, after flying in from Johannesburg where they had ostensibly been attending a charity tennis tournament. However, during their stay in South Africa they flew in a private Jet to the (then) Rhodesian border, where they were re-married by a local official in a private ceremony. This ended the 16-month separation which had terminated their first marriage. In 1976 Burton began drinking again and they broke up once more.

LEFT: Generalissimo Francisco Franco, dictator of Spain, died November 20 at the age of 82. His setting up of a far-right authoritarian regime in 1936 led to the Spanish Civil War in which his party received support from Mussolini and Hitler. Idealists from all over the world fought against the dictator but the regime remained until 1978. Franco's widow Carmen Polo de Franco, seen here, lived on until 1988.

OPPOSITE: Survivors of the Moorgate tube crash pictured in an ambulance, waiting to be taken to hospital. On February 28, a London Underground train traveling from Drayton Park on the Northern Line overshot the platform on arrival at Moorgate, plowing into a dead-end tunnel. More than 40 people, including the driver, died at the scene, while a number of others would subsequently lose their lives as a result of their injuries.

LEFT: A former Hollywood actor, Ronald Reagan held the position of Governor of California between 1967 and late 1974, and the following year he would announce his candidacy for presidential nomination for the second time in his political career. The party chose to back the incumbent, President Gerald Ford, in 1976 but Reagan had laid the groundwork for the 1980 campaign that would ultimately see him assume the presidency.

OPPOSITE: Entertainers Bing Crosby and Bob Hope. Avid golfers, Crosby and Hope built an enduring relationship both on and off screen, finding stardom with their series of *Road to ...* movies between 1940 and 1962. By the 1970s their film careers had slowed somewhat, although both remained active performers and broadcasters, with Crosby releasing four LPs in 1975.

1975

OPPOSITE: Stars of the BBC sitcom *Porridge*; the show was set in prison with the main characters sharing a cell. Ronnie Barker (left) and Richard Beckinsale played Norman Stanley Fletcher and Lennie Godber. First aired in 1974, *Porridge* (criminal slang for a jail sentence) began its second series in 1975 and would return for a third in 1977. At the same time, Beckinsale, father of the actress Kate Beckinsale, also played Alan Moore in the hit ITV sitcom *Rising Damp*, but in 1979 he would tragically die of a massive heart attack, aged just 31.

RIGHT: Felicity Kendal and Richard Briers as Barbara and Tom Good, in the BBC situation comedy *The Good Life*. The show was based on the Goods' attempt to adopt a sustainable, self-sufficient lifestyle, a premise that was perhaps influenced by the growing environmental movement, which gathered momentum during the 1970s after the United Nations Conference on the Human Environment and the publication of such works as *The Limits to Growth* and *Small Is Beautiful*.

ABOVE: Angie Dickinson's guest appearance in the NBC TV drama series *Police Story* landed her a four season show of her own: *Police Woman*, a weekly detective series in which she played Sgt. Leann "Pepper" Anderson in the LA Police Department. Dickinson married the composer Burt Bacharach in 1965; their daughter Nikki was born prematurely in 1961 and during the 15 year relationship with Bacharach her main focus was on the wellbeing of her daughter, leading to her turning down many roles that might have furthered her acting career.

OPPOSITE: 1975 saw the return to the silver screen of history's least competent police investigator—Blake Edwards' accident-prone Inspector Clouseau, played by Peter Sellers in *The Return of the Pink Panther*. As usual, the plot provided a framework for Clouseau's knockabout antics and strange pronunciations. Despite the levity of the subject matter, the Pink Panther movies were cleverly witty, and the acting and production excellent, including music by Henry Mancini.

1975

OPPOSITE: The aftermath of an IRA car bomb in Connaught Square, London, in November 1975. Throughout the year the IRA stepped up its mainland terror campaign, detonating explosives at various locations in London, including Oxford Street, the Hilton Hotel, and Scotts Restaurant in Mayfair. An off duty policeman was also fatally shot, and the TV personality and *Guinness Book of Records* founder Ross McWhirter was murdered after offering a £50,000 reward for information leading to the capture of those responsible.

ABOVE: Police officers with weapons drawn during the Balcombe Street Siege. Following a second attack at Scotts Restaurant, four members of an IRA active service unit were pursued by the police to a block of flats on Balcombe Street, London, where they holed up for almost a week, having taken two residents hostage. The "Balcombe Street Gang" eventually surrendered, and its members were subsequently all found guilty of murder. It later transpired that they had admitted to the Guildford pub bombings, although they were never charged with these offences.

Serial killer Peter Sutcliffe, nicknamed the Yorkshire Ripper, left school at the age of 15 and took on a series of menial jobs. During one spell as a gravedigger, he claimed God had spoken to him. He began his assaults on women in July 1975, using a hammer and blade. His first three victims survived his attack but the fourth, 28-year-old mother of four Wilma McCann, was killed on October 30. He murdered a total of 13 people before he was arrested in 1981 and sentenced to life imprisonment. He remains in Broadmoor Hospital—the UK's principal secure prison for the criminally insane.

American serial killer Ted Bundy pictured while serving his prison sentence prior to his execution by electric chair. During the years 1973 to 1978 Bundy is thought to have murdered more than 30 people. After two escapes from county jails, Bundy was finally apprehended in 1978 and was later sentenced to the death penalty.

ABOVE: Hysterical fans of Scottish pop group the Bay City Rollers, named after Bay City in Michigan. Formed in the late 1960s, the band enjoyed their first hits in the early 1970s, and by 1975 they were one of Britain's biggest-selling acts, reaching the top of the charts with the singles "Bye, Bye, Baby" and "Give a Little Love." "Saturday Night," their debut single in the US, reached the top spot on the *Billboard* Hot 100 in 1976.

OPPOSITE: Paul and Linda McCartney. 1975 was a busy year for Paul McCartney: the first album to be released by Wings under MPL Communications (Paul's own management company), *Venus And Mars,* was issued in May and later in the year the Wings Over the World tour kicked off with its first international leg in Australia.

1975

ABOVE: The leaders of the Khmer Rouge, Pol Pot, Noun Chea, Leng Sary, and Son Sen (pictured left to right, foreground) in Phnom Penh shortly after taking power following a long military uprising that started in 1968. The Communist regime sought to completely re-engineer Cambodian society with a program that left an estimated two million people dead.

OPPOSITE: Tanks on the streets of Luanda at the start of the Angolan Civil War in 1975. Angola's conflict, like many in Africa's modern history, was grounded in the colonial dividing up of the continent by external powers who ignored traditional geographic and ethnic boundaries. Twentieth century global adversaries US and Soviet Russia took over the vacuum left by the dissolving colonial administrations, making Africa in the 1960s and 1970s a theater for the Cold War. Countries such as Angola paid a terrible price for their mineral wealth, which made feudal chiefs and their western sponsors rich but wrecked the lives of common people.

1975

LEFT: In 1974 tennis star Jimmy Connors achieved number one world ranking, which he held for over three years, a record that he retained until it was broken by Roger Federer in 2007. Something of a maverick, Connors was not one to hold his emotions in check on the court. Seen here playing Raúl Ramírez in the quarter-final of 1975 Wimbledon Championships, he went on to lose to Arthur Ashe in the men's final. Connors was suing Ashe at the time but they settled out of court after Wimbledon.

OPPOSITE: Formula One Racing driver James Hunt takes a spin on his motorbike. Looking more like a tourist than a champion, Hunt was the perfect driver for the team assembled by private owner Lord Hesketh; beneath a façade of upper-class English privilege, the team was more competitive than it appeared. As for Hunt, T-shirt and jeans was his favored dress code even on formal occasions.

1975

LEFT: Suzi Quatro released her third album, *Your Mama Won't Like Me,* in 1975. An American brought up in a musical family, Quatro settled in the UK in 1971 and was launched onto the glam rock scene by London promoter Mickie Most, producer of The Animals, Jeff Beck, Lulu, and Donovan. Quatro's powerful vocal delivery and swaggering stage performance got her a better reaction to her music in the UK than in her native USA despite touring with Alice Cooper. In the USA she's better known for her cameo role in the TV show *Happy Days*.

OPPOSITE: After two notable albums in the early 1970s, Bob Marley's band the Wailers broke up, leaving him to re-form as Bob Marley and the Wailers; 1975 was his breakthrough year with hit single "No Woman No Cry" leading to a US hit album, *Rastaman Vibration*, the following year. Marley's rousing ballads with their sensual beat lived on after his early death at the age of 36, making him one of rock's great legends.

1976

British Prime Minister
Harold Wilson leaves
10 Downing Street after
his sensational resignation
announcement made on March
16, 1976. The resignation
came completely out of the
blue, stunning his own cabinet
colleagues and politicians
everywhere throughout Britain.
He explained that, after his
election victory in 1974, he had
decided he would only stay
in office for two years, and
"I have not wavered in this
decision."

241

Starsky and Hutch, the TV police drama set in urban southern California and shot mostly in San Pedro, starred David Soul as Detective Ken "Hutch" Hutchinson and Paul Michael Glaser as Detective David Starsky. Screening began in April on ABC and was characterized by the close bond of the two detectives, their colorful Gran Torino car, and lots of violent crime. Over four seasons 93 episodes were broadcast. Outside of USA the show was a big hit in Europe, bought by BBC1 and later re-run over other networks, bringing it a large audience. At the same time, David Soul was also enjoying a successful career in music, topping the charts on both sides of the Atlantic with the single "Don't Give Up on Us."

Jim Henson's TV puppet show *Sesame Street* put him on the map for kids, but he wanted to expand his audience to an older target group. When Lew Grade, head of British broacast company ATV, offered him a contract, Henson signed up and started making *The Muppet Show* in Elstree Studios, England. The first show went out in September and its zany puppet cast, with Kermit the Frog and Miss Piggy center stage, quickly won the affection of a broad audience both sides of the Atlantic. Slapstick, chaos, and funny voices (often set to music) were the key characteristics. Surprisingly the show attracted major celebrities to participate in the mayhem. Zoot, the minimalist and cool sax player, is pictured here. One hundred and twenty episodes were made before the show ceased in 1981.

1976

ABOVE: Batsman Murray for the famed West Indies cricket team is clean bowled by England's John Snow during the second day of the second Test at Lord's cricket ground in 1976.

OPPOSITE: Olga Korbut, the diminutive Russian gymnast who stole the hearts of the crowd at the 1972 Munich Olympic Games and came away with three gold medals. She returned to take another gold at the Montreal Olympics in 1976 but retired from the scene after this to become coach to the Soviet team.

1976

ABOVE: On September 17, 1976, the space shuttle *Enterprise*, the test prototype for NASA's Space Transportation System, was rolled out of Rockwell's plant at Palmdale, California. In recognition of its *Star Trek* namesake, creator Gene Roddenberry and most of the cast of the original series of *Star Trek* were invited to the dedication ceremony. *Enterprise* was used for atmospheric testing and did not undertake a space mission; it now occupies pride of place in the Smithsonian's National Air and Space Museum in Washington, DC.

OPPOSITE: Following months of low rainfall, in 1976 Britain experienced one of the hottest, driest summers on record, and for over two weeks from late June to early July, temperatures exceeded 90°F in parts of the UK, with absolutely no rainfall in some areas. South Wales and southern England were particularly badly affected, with the soaring heat sparking forest fires and water shortages. Here residents of Northam, Devon, stand in line to collect water from a standpipe.

As part of the USA's Bicentennial celebrations in 1976, 16 tall ships took part in the Parade of Ships, sailing up the Hudson River in New York City on the Fourth of July and then onwards to Boston a week later. Here, in a view over New York's Pier 84, are pictured the Argentine *Libertad* (left) and the Japanese *Nippon Maru* (center right). The ships are used as training vessels and participate in the Tall Ships races; when seen together these vintage vessels are a breathtaking sight.

1976

OPPOSITE: Jaclyn Smith, Farrah Fawcett-Majors, and Kate Jackson, stars of the US TV series *Charlie's Angels*, which launched in 1976. The show was one of the first to feature women in parts usually portrayed by men.

RIGHT: Actor Leonard Rossiter in a scene from the British sitcom *The Fall and Rise of Reginald Perrin*, which first aired in 1976, and concerned the mental decline of a suburban sales executive, who sought to escape the pressures of an unfulfilling job and dysfunctional home life. The character eventually attempts to fake his own death by abandoning his clothes on a beach, in uncanny resemblance to the real-life actions of the MP John Stonehouse, who fled to Australia in the mid 1970s.

1976

ABOVE: Democratic candidate Jimmy Carter pictured relaxing during a softball game in Plains, Georgia. A former peanut farmer, Carter held the position of Governor of Georgia from 1971 to 1975, but was relatively unknown when he decided to run for president in 1976. Nevertheless, in November of that year, he was elected as the 39th President of the United States, having campaigned against the corruption in Washington that had been unearthed by the Watergate scandal.

OPPOSITE: Edward Heath with new Conservative Party leader Margaret Thatcher at her first party conference as leader, in Brighton in October. There was no love lost between the two and Heath never forgave her for ousting him as leader, leading to a long-standing feud, with Heath sniping from the Tory backbenches during Thatcher's premiereship.

1976

ABOVE: Composer Andrew Lloyd Webber pictured during the recording of *Evita*, his musical about the Argentinian First Lady, Eva Perón. As with *Jesus Christ Superstar*, the project was a collaboration between Lloyd Webber and lyricist Tim Rice and first emerged as a concept album before being staged as a musical. The album was released in 1976 and spawned the number one single "Don't Cry for Me Argentina," sung by Julie Covington.

OPPOSITE: Radio One disk jockey and children's TV presenter Ed "Stewpot" Stewart pictured with Sandra Bain, the winner of the national space hopper championships. Introduced by the Italian rubber-ball manufacturer Ledragomma in the late 1960s, the bouncing toy, which was also known as a "kangaroo ball," sparked a huge craze in Britain and the US in the early 1970s, and continued to remain a firm favorite with children throughout the decade.

1976

Actress Joanna Lumley filming *The New Avengers* at Pinewood Studios. The series gave the former model her first major acting role, as Purdy, although she had previously enjoyed a small part in the 1969 James Bond film *On Her Majesty's Secret Service*, and appearances in *Coronation Street, Steptoe and Son,* and *Are You Being Served?*. The star of the original *Avengers* series, Patrick Mcnee, revived his role as John Steed in *The New Avengers*, while the more youthful Gareth Hunt was brought in to play tough guy Mike Gambit.

Brotherhood of Man performing in the 1976 Song for Europe contest, which would see them selected as the British entrant for the Eurovision Song Contest that year. The group, which consisted of Nicky Stevens, Sandra Stevens, Martin Lee, and Lee Sheridan, went on to win the competition with the song "Save Your Kisses for Me," which subsequently topped the UK charts for some six weeks, and reinvigorated the group's career.

ABOVE: Although it was first flown in test flights as early as 1969, the supersonic jet aircraft Concorde did not enter service until 1976, with the inaugural British Airways flight being made from London to Bahrain on January 21 (pictured). In the US there were concerns over potential noise pollution from sonic booms, but special permission was granted for transatlantic flights to Washington in May, and by 1977 services from Paris and London were also flying into New York.

OPPOSITE: Romanian tennis star Ilie Nastase in action at Wimbledon. A former world number one, Nastase was ranked third behind his friend and doubles partner Jimmy Connors and Sweden's Bjorn Borg in 1976, and although he would make it to the singles final at Wimbledon, he would lose out to Borg, who would effectively come to dominate both that tournament and the French Open for the rest of the decade.

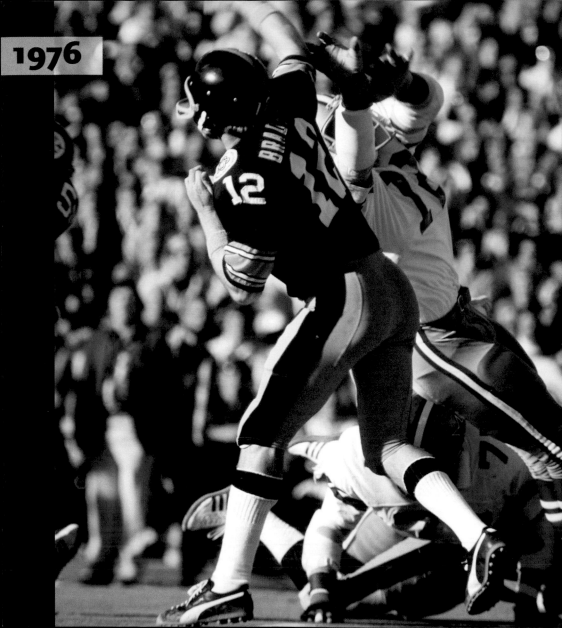

OPPOSITE: Quarterback Terry Bradshaw of the Pittsburgh Steelers passes under the pressure of the Dallas Cowboys defense during Super Bowl X at the Orange Bowl, Miami, on January 18. The Steelers defeated the Cowboys 21-17.

ABOVE: Premier flat racing competition in the UK, the Triple Crown starts with Royal Ascot's Gold Cup, held on Ladies' Day during Royal Ascot Week in June, with the winner receiving the prize from the Queen. In 1976 the crowds cheered Sagaro, ridden by Lester Piggot to the finishing line for the second year in a row; the success would be repeated the following year, making a record that would last until 2009.

1976

RIGHT: Britain's most wanted man, Donald Neilson, commonly known as "the Black Panther." Born Donald Nappey on August 1, 1936, Neilson was jailed for life in July 1976 for the murder of 17-year-old Shropshire heiress Lesley Whittle and three sub-postmasters in post office robberies.

OPPOSITE: The Ugandan President and military dictator Idi Amin, pictured with journalist Ian Wooldridge. In 1976 international relations with Uganda, which were already seriously strained, were further damaged after Amin permitted the landing of a hijacked Air France plane at Entebbe Airport. The Palestinian and German terrorists released most of the passengers, but detained all Jews and Israelis, most of whom were subsequently freed in a daring rescue mission by Israeli commandos.

1976

OPPOSITE: Actress Lindsay Wagner had numerous small movie and TV roles until she took the part of Jaime Sommers, the sweetheart of the Six Million Dollar Man, Steve Austin, in a two part special called *The Bionic Woman*. Wagner's character was rebuilt bionically after a skydiving accident but tragically died when her bionic transplants were rejected. This was no obstacle to the studios, who brought Jaime Sommers out of cryonic suspension and gave her a show of her own, *The Bionic Woman*, which ran from 1976 for three seasons and 57 episodes.

RIGHT: Charlotte Cornwell, Julie Covington, and Rula Lenska, as Anna Ward, Devonia "Dee" Rhoades, and Nancy 'Q' Cunard de Longchamps in the innovative musical comedy drama *Rock Follies*, which traced the fortunes of the fictional girl band The Little Ladies. The show won a BAFTA in 1976, while a spin-off LP achieved the rare feat of entering the UK album charts at number one that same year.

ABOVE: Presdent Gerald Ford, flanked by Secretary of State Henry Kissinger, left, and Secretary of Defense Donald Rumsfeld, right, holds his first post-election cabinet meeting in the White House. Historic documents obtained by the Associated Press showed that an intense debate erupted during the Ford Administration, with key arguments by George H.W. Bush and Donald Rumsfeld, over the President's powers to eavesdrop without warrants for foreign intelligence purposes. In the foreground are Attorney General Edward Levi (left) and Vice President Nelson Rockefeller (right).

OPPOSITE: Henry Kissinger, the American Secretary of State, at an American Embassy press conference. Kissinger played a pivotal role in world affairs and was constantly in the public eye. In 1973 he was awarded the Nobel Peace Prize for his role in the Paris Peace Accords, laying the foundation for ending the Vietnam War. In contradiction to this was Kissinger's more covert involvement of the US in South American affairs—particularly in Chile and Argentina and farther afield in Africa. The US would pay heavily in future for its foreign policy in the 1970s. Interestingly, Kissinger was a valued informal advisor to President George W. Bush on Middle East affairs.

1976

OPPOSITE: Jodie Foster in 1976 at Pinewood Studios, England, where she was making the musical gangster spoof *Bugsy Malone*, a far cry from her stark performance in Scorsese's *Taxi Driver*, which she had made the previous year, aged just 13.

OPPOSITE: Robert De Niro received excellent notices for his performances in Scorsese's *Mean Streets* (1973) and Coppola's *The Godfather: Part II* (1974), winning an award for Best Supporting Actor, two years after Marlon Brando had won Best Actor for the role and the only time two actors have received Oscars for the same part. However, it was De Niro's portrayal of Travis Bickle in 1976's *Taxi Driver* (again directed by Scorsese) that really demonstrated his talent.

Johnny Rotten of the Sex Pistols performing at one of the last gigs of their UK tour. In October EMI signed them up for a two year contract; musically they were raucous and loud with angry lyrics in discordant tunes. Punk rock said everything about the social bleakness of the early 1970s and the anger of the young generation of the time, which was also displayed in the aggressive pogo-ing dance of the audiences and the spitting tradition at gigs. The Pistols' first single, "Anarchy in the UK," was released at the end of November, reaching number 38 in the UK singles chart.

ABOVE: Director Sam Peckinpah (right) pictured in a caravan at Elstree Studios with actor James Coburn during the making of the movie Cross of Iron. The pair had previously worked together on the productions Major Dundee and Pat Garrett & Billy the Kid, both of which were beset with problems, and funds would similarly run out during the filming of Cross of Iron. Peckinpah was drinking heavily at this time but despite these setbacks his film was released to critical acclaim in Europe.

OPPOSITE: Fat Sam, owner of the eponymous club in Alan Parker's first feature film, Bugsy Malone, is pictured here with his henchmen. Parker's spoof of the gangster world of 1930s Prohibition America used a juvenile cast of mainly unknown actors. The movie was a musical with score by Paul Williams, who was renowned for some of the decade's greatest hits by stars such as the Carpenters—his work earned the movie its only Oscar. Loved by kids for the music and the "splurge guns," the film was a modest box office success but lives on as a cinema classic.

1977

Woody Allen's 1977 movie
Annie Hall moved him into the
mainstream of success as a writer,
director, and actor—although his
films retained a distinctive style.
The film picked up four Academy
Awards and introduced Diane
Keaton (opposite) as the thinking
man's sex symbol, at the same
time creating a new fashion in
women's headgear. Allen, in this
film and others, milks his own
character's intellectual agonies and
sophisticated if neurotic humor,
giving his movies a recurring
focus on the ambiguities of life,
relationships, and sexual failure.

1977

LEFT: Singer Debbie Harry of the American new wave pop group Blondie, pictured in concert, June 1977. This was Blondie's breakout year: their debut album *Blondie* was re-released in the USA after UK label Chrysalis Records bought their US record company. The same year *Rolling Stone* magazine noticed them for the first time—this, combined with a surge of popularity on their Australian tour and release of a second album, led to chart-topping success.

OPPOSITE: Punk rockers in party mood in a Soho nightclub in 1977, swearing, spitting, and smashing beer glasses.

ABOVE: June 1977: The week of festivities celebrating the Silver Jubilee of Queen Elizabeth II's accession to the throne began with the Queen lighting a giant bonfire in Windsor Great Park. It was the first of 100 beacons that lit the skies all around the country. People all over Britain celebrated by holding street parties, and when the Queen attended the thanksgiving service at St. Paul's Cathedral, over a million people lined the procession route. Wherever she went the Queen was met with enthusiasm and great warmth. To mark the anniversary, she undertook an extensive tour of the world.

OPPOSITE: The Queen and Prince Philip kneel in St. Paul's Cathedral during the thankgsiving service attended by heads of state from around the world as well as members of British government and former prime ministers.

ABOVE: British broadcaster David Frost with disgraced former president Richard Nixon. After two years as a virtual recluse Nixon was pushed back into the public eye by his publicist, who thought he could recover favor. Frost's bid of $600,000 and 20 percent of profits from broadcasts won the right to intensively interview Richard Nixon. The interviews ran to over 28 hours and were made into four 90 minute programs, broadcast during May. The story of the Frost/Nixon interviews was later the subject of a play, then a movie, *Frost/Nixon,* released in 2008.

OPPOSITE: LeVar Burton plays the central role of Kunta Kinte in the ABC TV drama series *Roots*, which traces the ancestry of an African American family from the capture and enslavement of Kinte, a Mandinka from Gambia, West Africa, born in 1750, to the emancipation of his descendants after the American Civil War. The saga was based on a novel by Alex Haley. The 12 hour, eight episode mini-series, screened on consecutive nights in January, set US audience-rating records and won nine Emmys and a Golden Globe.

1977

LEFT: Emlyn Hughes, Liverpool's captain, holds the European Cup high in jubilation after the team's emphatic 3–1 victory over the German side Borussia Moenchengladbach.

OPPOSITE: Fourteen-year-old Tracy Austin made her first appearance in a Grand Slam tournament at Wimbledon in 1977. Austin lost to Chris Evert in the third round but was to win her first Grand Slam title two years later when she defeated Evert in the final of the US Open.

1977

OPPOSITE: In 1976 workers at the Grunwick Film Processing Laboratories in north London were unhappy with their conditions of employment and chose to join the union APEX. Those who did so (mainly female and Asian) were then fired by their employer. The Grunwick dispute rapidly became a cause celebre for the unionized workforce across the country and the Trades Union Conference (TUC) called for sympathetic action from other union members. Pictured here is miners' leader Arthur Scargill arriving at Grunwick in 1977 to lend his support to protesting picketers. The public face of union militancy in the 1970s, Scargill's appearance would guarantee publicity. So-called "secondary picketing" led to violent clashes with police when the picket tried to prevent Grunwick staff entering the premises.

RIGHT: The scene in Willesden High Street after the pickets had clashed with police.

1977

Jockey Jean Grugent sits atop of Seattle Slew, racing in the lead in the Kentucky Derby at Churchill Downs, Louisville, Kentucky, on May 7, 1977. Two weeks later they also won the Preakness Stakes at the Pimlico Race course in Baltimore. Seattle Slew became the tenth American Triple Crown Winner when he was also victorious in the Belmont Stakes. In 1978 Affirmed repeated the feat, becoming the 11th, and to date last, winner of the Triple Crown.

1977

ABOVE: British comedy duo Eric Morecambe and Ernie Wise, pictured performing in *The Morecambe and Wise Christmas Show* in 1977. Broadcast on Christmas Day, the program attracted an audience of around 28 million viewers, which, at around half the UK population, made it one of the most successful programs of all time.

OPPOSITE: In 1977 Arnold Schwarzenegger was little known outside the bodybuilding community, where he had been winning competitions from age 18. In 1970 he won "Mr Olympia" at 23—the youngest ever winner. 1977 found Arnie in London with a new movie, *Pumping Iron*, and a book on bodybuilding to promote. Although the documentary, behind-the-scenes style of *Pumping Iron* boosted his career, it would be the next decade when Arnie got his breakout opportunity in the movies.

1977

ABOVE: Having first peaked in popularity around 1965, skateboarding underwent a major resurgence during the 1970s, with a host of developments taking place in both technology and technique. The introduction of polyurethane wheels, specialized axles or trucks, and wider decks coincided with the evolution of new tricks and styles, such as vert skating, and heralded the advent of the sport's first major stars, including Tony Alva, Jay Adams, and Stacy Peralta.

OPPOSITE: The 1970s brought the rise of disco culture, whose club style went on wheels in the form of Roller Disco. These girls are enjoying the last days of the current fad, soon to be replaced by the invention of in-line skates, or "Rollerblades," which would peak in the 1980s and 1990s, making street skating even more fashionable.

ABOVE: The remains of a KLM jumbo jet at Los Rodeos Airport, Santa Cruz de Tenerife, in March 1977. The world's worst air disaster killed 583 people when KLM Flight 4805 crashed into taxiing Pan Am Flight 1736 as the KLM airplan attempted to take off. The Tenerife airport was crowded with diverted planes following detonation of a terrorist bomb at Las Palmas' main airport for the Canary Islands. The weather was very foggy and not only could the aircraft not see each other, the control tower did not have visibility over the runway and there was no ground radar equipment. Although too late for the victims, the lessons learned from the tragedy led to widespread changes in operating procedures in airlines around the world.

OPPOSITE: August 18: fans watch as a white hearse, escorted by a cortege of 49 cars, carries Elvis's body to the Forest Hills Cemetery.

ABOVE: World chess champion Anatoly Karpov of Russia in action against 12-year-old Nigel Short during a junior tournament. Karpov became world champion in 1975 when Bobby Fischer was forced to relinquish the title and retained the crown until 1985, when fellow Russian Garry Kasparov narrowly defeated him.

OPPOSITE: Russian ballet dancer Rudolf Nureyev with Patricia Ruanne. In 1977 Ruanne began a long and formative working relationship with Nureyev when he chose her for the role of Juliet in his groundbreaking production of Prokofiev's *Romeo and Juliet*, which premiered at the London Coliseum on June 2. That same year, Nureyev also played the lead in Ken Russell's film *Valentino*, which proved to be a critical and commercial failure.

1977

Womens VOICE NOISS

NO RETURN TO BACKSTREET ABORTION

NO RETURN TO BACKSTREET

FREE ABORTION ON DEMAND

OPPOSITE: The 70s marked the rise of feminism, following the spread of seminal ideas like those of Germaine Greer in her bestselling *The Female Eunuch*. The Women's Liberation Movement claimed the right to enjoy the same social and sexual freedoms as men. Abortion was legalized in Britain in 1967 but a heated debate continued across Europe and in the US through the 70s as pro-life and pro-abortion supporters tried to persuade governments to alter laws in their favor.

RIGHT: The feminists may have been eschewing traditional feminine charms, burning bras and setting free underarm hair, but glamour was alive and well in the Miss World competition. Seen here is Mary Stavin, Swedish winner of the 1977 contest; demure by modern standards, she fulfilled a more conventional role as George Best's girlfriend and as a Bond girl.

1977

Barbara Knox as Rita Littlewood and Peter Adamson as Len Fairclough, pictured on their wedding day in the British soap opera *Coronation Street*. Hugely popular since the early 1960s, ten years on viewing figures had slumped considerably as several key cast members left the show. However, the program's fortunes were revived by 1977, and the Fairclough wedding was a major event, warranting a two-part TV special and a pull-out feature in *TV Times* magazine.

The cast of the musical *A Chorus Line*, including Donna McKechnie as Cassie (front right). Launched in 1976, the original production was a huge success, winning nine Tony Awards and the Pulitzer Prize for drama, while McKechnie would earn her several awards of her own. In 1980 she was forced to stop dancing due to severe arthritis, but following treatment, she returned to the Broadway production of *A Chorus Line* in 1986.

1977

OPPOSITE: Luke Skywalker (Mark Hamill), Princess Leia (Carrie Fisher), and Han Solo (Harrison Ford) are three of the protagonists in *Star Wars*, a galactic space epic written and directed by George Lucas. As well as the epic plot and exotic characters, the movie used new visual technologies to astonish its audience, from the introductory sequence to the final credits, all orchestrated with unforgettable musical score by John Williams. LucasFilm, George Lucas' production company, set up the specialist Industrial Light & Magic, to achieve the special effects that imaginatively powered the movie, which became an instant box office hit, spawning two sequels spaced over the next six years.

ABOVE: Mengistu Haile Mariam, who seized power in Ethiopia in February 1977, and Cuban President Fidel Castro ride in an open car through the streets of Addis Ababa. Mengistu Haile Mariam was the top official of the Soviet-backed Derg party which overthrew Emperor Haile Selassie, while Castro was one of the Ethiopian regime's most important allies, and sent thousands of men to help Ethiopia defeat

1977

ABOVE: Fleetwood Mac epitomized the bohemian style of 70s musicians. The band went through many permutations in its history but was formed under the paternal eye of blues legend John Mayall, while founder member Peter Green was still around. Here is pictured the 1977 lineup: (left to right) Mick Fleetwood, Stevie Nicks, John McVie, Christine McVie, and Lindsey Buckingham. The band's 1977 album *Rumors* won Grammy for Album of the Year. It reflected the turmoil in the lives of the band members at the time. The pain was worth it: *Rumors* would be one of the bestselling albums of all time.

OPPOSITE: *The Spy Who Loved Me* was the tenth James Bond movie and the third to star Roger Moore as 007. Opposite him as female star was Barbara Bach in the role of KGB agent Anya Amasova. The bad guys are played by Curd Juergens and metal-fanged "Jaws," Richard Kiel, who, at over 7 feet tall, towered over Moore, hardly short at 6 foot 2 inches.

1978

Paul Weller, Rick Buckler, and Bruce Foxton, new wave band The Jam, released their new album *All Mod Cons*—a play on their dress style, inspired by the likes of The Who and Steve Marriott, performing in suits and with neat haircuts in contrast to their punk contemporaries. 1978 was their breakout year and established them as leaders of a particular style of English rock music with a strong social theme that they, and especially Weller, would champion in years to come.

1978

LEFT: A "punk" on the King's Road in Chelsea. Punk rockers made a point of looking as rebellious and outlandish as possible. Their devil-may-care attitude often led to clashes with other groups.

OPPOSITE: A punk rocker with one of the more exuberant hair styles at Piccadilly Circus, London. Although starting out as the antithesis of fashion, punks worked hard on their image and like this young woman enjoyed being a spectacle for London tourists.

1978

RIGHT: Robert De Niro in *The Deer Hunter*, the noted Michael Cimino movie which tracks the Vietnam War experiences of three friends. A complex emotional drama in a devastating setting, the title is derived from an epiphanic moment when De Niro deliberately misses a beautiful deer held in the sights of his rifle. The movie also starred Christopher Walken, Meryl Streep, and John Cazale; it won five Academy Awards. The horrific experience of Vietnam simulated in the movie was in contrast to its distinctive and emotionally charged theme music, "Cavatina," composed by Stanley Myers and performed by John Williams on classical guitar.

OPPOSITE: Husband and wife acting team Charles Bronson and Jill Ireland, who married in 1968 and starred in numerous movies together, including *Rider on the Train*, *Città Violenta*, *Breakheart Pass*, and 1978's *Love and Bullets*. The screenplay was written by Wendell Mayes, who had also worked on the 1974 Bronson movie *Death Wish*.

1978

LEFT: In November 1977 English firemen went on strike and 60,000 of them marched on Downing Street. They took with them a petition with half a million signatures calling on Prime Minister Jim Callaghan to agree to their wage demands.

OPPOSITE: Firemen picketing the fire station at Chelsea read messages of support.

ABOVE: Elton John performing in 1978. Despite having retreated from the spotlight, Elton made a handful of low-key live appearances, including a two hour concert at the MCA National Convention in California to promote the LP *A Single Man*.

OPPOSITE: Musician and entertainer Liberace making a guest appearance on *The Muppet Show*, where he notably performed a version of "Chopsticks." Born in a modest Polish-Italian household, Liberace showed early talent at the piano and went on to become one of America's best-known entertainers with his popular TV show and his regular touring. Liberace's flamboyant and camp stage style was underlaid with a charming personality and he was a gay icon—one whom Elton John, for instance, regarded as a role model. Liberace denied being a homosexual but would die from complications arising from AIDS in 1987.

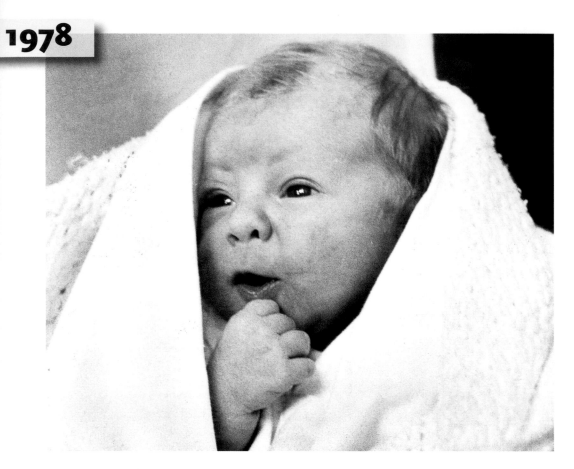

ABOVE: The world's first "test tube" baby, Louise Brown, was born by a Cesarean section at Oldham District General Hospital, July 25, 1978. Patrick Steptoe, a pioneer of in vitro fertilization, had spent more than 12 years perfecting the technique along with fellow scientist Robert Edwards.

OPPOSITE: The 1970s were golden years for operatic tenor Luciano Pavarotti, pictured here with Australian soprano Joan Sutherland, whose collaboration helped launch Pavarotti's career in the 1960s. Both singers were at the height of their careers at this time, earning Pavarotti a place on the front cover of *Time* magazine in 1977.

1978

ABOVE: US President Jimmy Carter walks up London's Whitehall to the Banqueting Hall, alongside French President Giscard d'Estaing and Germany's Chancellor Helmut Schmidt. In September 1978 Carter was praised by world leaders for bringing together the two warring nations of Egypt and Israel at Camp David. The peace treaty was signed by Anwar Sadat and Menachem Begin. Begin said that Carter had 'worked harder than our forefathers did in Egypt building the pyramids'.

OPPOSITE: Pope Paul VI died in August 1978 and was succeeded by Pope John Paul I, whose Vatican office lasted barely a month. Polish Cardinal Karol Jozef Wojtyla was elected by the conclave and chose the name Pope John Paul II; he was destined to be one of the longest-serving pontiffs. His many travels over the world extended the influence of the Vatican and its traditional orthodoxy. Seen here in St. Peter's Square, John Paul II's interaction with the crowd in such open vehicles ended after an assassination attempt in May 1981.

1978

RIGHT: Bjorn Borg holds up the Wimbledon singles trophy for the third consecutive time in July 1978, having beaten Jimmy Connors in one of the greatest finals the tournament had ever seen. The last man to perform the feat was Fred Perry in 1934, 1935, and 1936.

OPPOSITE: Popular Spanish golfer Severiano Ballesteros turned professional in 1974, aged 16, and made his mark at the 1976 Open at Royal Birkdale when the tied with Jack Nicklaus for second place. Ballesteros went on to win the Open in 1979, 1984, and 1988, the Masters in 1980 and 1983, and was a member of five winning Ryder Cup teams before he retired in because of problems with his back.

1978

RIGHT: Elaine Paige as Eva Perón in the Andrew Lloyd Webber and Tim Rice musical *Evita*. Paige had performed in numerous West End musicals during the early 1970s, including *Hair*, *Jesus Christ Superstar*, *Grease*, *Billy,* and *The Boy Friend*, but despite this she was still relatively unknown when she was cast in the original production of *Evita* in 1978. Madonna took the title role in the 1996 movie of the musical.

OPPOSITE: Jackie O. After the death of her second husband, Aristotle Onassis, Jackie began a new life in New York, taking a job in a publishing house and finding love with diamond merchant Maurice Tempelsman.

ABOVE: Disk jockey Dave Lee Travis, setting his alarm clock after it was announced he would be taking over the breakfast show on Radio One following Noel Edmonds' departure from the program at the end of April. "DLT," or "the Hairy Monster" as he became known, started out with BBC Radio One in 1968 and ended in August 1993 when he famously announced his resignation live on air, telling his audience he disagreed with changes being made to the station, which "go against my principles."

OPPOSITE: Eric Clapton had recovered from drug addiction but by 1978 he was drinking heavily and this would regularly affect his performance. Drinking contributed to the breakup of his relationship with Pattie Boyd, though it was a new love of Eric's that was the ultimate trigger. At the end of 1978 Clapton and his band were touring Europe to promote the album *Backless*. The band traveled by rail, in three cars that used to be part of Hermann Goering's private train.

1978

ABOVE: The environmental campaigning organization Greenpeace acquired the former trawler *Sir William Hardy* in 1977; she was refitted and relaunched as *Rainbow Warrior* in spring 1978. The vessel led protests against whaling, sealing, and nuclear testing. It was during the latter action in 1985 that she was sunk by a French intelligence team while in harbor in New Zealand, creating an international scandal.

OPPOSITE: Labour Prime Minister James Callaghan meets President Anwar el-Sadat of Egypt in 1978. During his presidency, Sadat initiated the Yom Kippur War against Israel, and his reclamation of part of the Sinai Desert for Egypt made him a hero of the Arab world. However, he later made strenuous attempts at peace with Israel, probably the reason why he was later assassinated by fundamentalists in his own country in 1981. As well as meeting Callaghan in London he traveled to Germany for talks with Chancellor Schmidt. All this was leading up to the historic Camp David Accords in September, which were the foundation for peace in the Middle East.

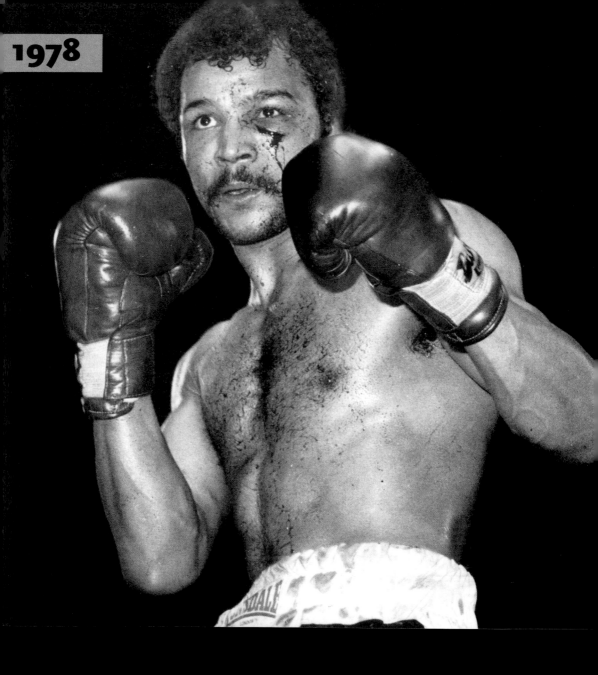

RIGHT: At 18 years old, in 1975 Martina Navratilova made it to the final in both the Australian Open, losing to Evonne Goolagong Cawley, and the French Open, losing to Chris Evert. In 1978 Navratilova scored her first Grand Slam victory and world number one ranking by defeating Evert to win the women's singles title at Wimbledon, a feat that she would repeat the following year. Also in 1978, Navratilova scored a victory in the US Open, partnering Billie Jean King in the women's doubles.

OPPOSITE: WBC World Light Heavyweight Champion John Conteh. One of Britain's most successful boxers, in 1973, at the age of just 21, Conteh held the British, Commonwealth, and European titles, and the following year he would win the world title after defeating Argentinean Jorge Ahumada at Wembley. Conteh went on to successfully defend the world title on three occasions, but he was stripped of his crown in 1978 after failing to mount a mandatory defense in Monte Carlo.

A scene from the classic British sitcom *Rising Damp*, which starred Frances de la Tour as Miss Jones, Leonard Rossiter as Rigsby, and Don Warrington as Philip. Adapted by Eric Chappell from his play *The Banana Box*, in which the lead actors had all appeared in 1973, the program ran for four series between 1974 and 1978, with the final series commanding huge audiences of more than 18 million viewers. The show also won a BAFTA in 1978 for Best Situation Comedy.

Ronnie Corbett (left) and Ronnie Barker in a sketch from their BBC TV comedy show *The Two Ronnies*, which was broadcast over 12 series between 1971 and 1986. When *The Morecambe and Wise Show* moved from the BBC to Thames Television in 1978, *The Two Ronnies* became the BBC's leading comedy program and, at the height of its popularity, regularly attracted viewing audiences of over 17 million.

LEFT: Former First Lady Betty Ford poses in front of her portrait. She married Gerald Ford in 1948 and he became President in 1974, taking over from disgraced Richard Nixon. Betty was a very active and modern thinking First Lady, openly supporting social change, especially in the area of women's rights. In 1978, under pressure from her family, she confronted her alcoholism and dependency on prescription painkillers which she had been taking since the 1960s. After her rehabilitation, she founded the Betty Ford Center, making her name a byword, especially among celebrities, for recovery from alcohol or drug dependency.

OPPOSITE: The movie *Coma* starred Genevieve Bujold and Michael Douglas in a hybrid of sci-fi, medical drama, and horror. Director Michael Crichton indulged his favorite passions, unraveling a plot in a normal-looking hospital to harvest organs from murdered surgery cases and sell them to clients around the world. The rank of living corpses pictured here, hooked up to their life support systems, was the dominating image of the movie.

1978

LEFT: British golfer Nick Faldo in action at the European Open at Walton Heath, Surrey, in 1978. Having turned professional in 1976, Faldo impressed at the European Open, and at one point took the lead, although he would eventually finish fourth, behind Bobby Wadkins, Bernard Gallacher, and Gil Morgan. Nevertheless, Faldo won the PGA Championship event that year and finished third on the European Tour Order of Merit. His first major title came in 1987 at the British Open, and from the late 1980s to the early 1990s Faldo was regarded as one of the world's best golfers.

OPPOSITE: Liverpool defender Alan Hansen, pictured in the bath with the European Cup. Having received a bye into the second round, Liverpool FC defeated Dynamo Dresden, Benfica, and Borussia Mönchengladbach to get to the 1978 final at Wembley Stadium, where they beat Belgian side Club Brugge 1–0, to claim a second consecutive European Cup title.

The trophy bears the inscription "...les Clubs Champions Européens"

1978

ABOVE: Minnesota senator Walter Mondale was Jimmy Carter's running mate in the 1976 election and served as Vice-President of the United States between 1977 and 1981. Mondale secured the Democratic nomination in 1980 but was defeated by Ronald Reagan and retired from politics shortly afterward.

OPPOSITE: The supertanker *Amoco Cadiz* disappears beneath the waves off the coast of Brittany, France, in April 1978. Having sustained rudder damage in heavy seas, en route from the Persian Gulf to Rotterdam, the *Amoco Cadiz* ran aground on Portsall Rocks, and subsequently broke apart, shedding its cargo of over one million barrels of crude oil into the English Channel. This resulted in one of the biggest oil spills in history, which devastated wildlife both in the water and along a large expanse of shoreline.

ABOVE: James Garner (right) and Noah Beery, Jr., play down-at-heel private detective Jim Rockford and his father Rocky in NBC's hit show *The Rockford Files*, which aired between 1974 and 1980.

OPPOSITE: Noel Edmonds (right) and John Craven, presenters of the highly successful Saturday morning television program *Multi-Coloured Swap Shop*, which ran from 1976 to 1982. Maggie Philbin joined the team in 1978, and she would later marry co-presenter Keith Chegwin, who usually fronted the "Swaporama" outside broadcasts, where children could exchange their toys and possessions with each other. The show was notable for being broadcast live, and established a format for subsequent Saturday morning children's TV programs on the BBC.

ABOVE: Nottingham Forest manager Brian Clough leads his team in song as they rehearse for a recording of "We've Got the Whole World in Our Hands." At the top of their game in 1978, the team cut the record as they chased the First Division, FA Cup and the League Cup titles. The team came top of the First Division and won the League Cup but their record would only peak at number 24 in the UK charts.

OPPOSITE: Somerset and England all-round cricketer Ian Botham. In 1978 22-year-old Botham bowled England to victory in the second Test against Pakistan at Trent Bridge, and entered the record books by becoming the first player to both score a century and take eight wickets during a Test. Prior to this, the only England player to score a century and take more than five wickets was former captain Tony Greig. As a result, Botham was named one of *Wisden*'s five Cricketers of the Year.

ABOVE: Michael Douglas relaxes in the south of France after completing his most recent production, *The China Syndrome*. Douglas was now established as a producer, and would go on to have further success with his next two ventures, *Romancing the Stone* (1984) and *Jewel of the Nile* (1985), in which he also acted, alongside Danny DeVito and Kathleen Turner.

OPPOSITE: In 1978 John Travolta was to dominate the box office with two films, the disco-centric *Saturday Night Fever* and the 1950s pastiche *Grease*. Both were panned by the critics, but their success was ensured by the crowds that flocked to see them. Travolta became an overnight sensation among the young, but at the time lacked a vehicle and perhaps the gravitas that would carry him forward. In 1989 he would make the first of the *Look Who's Talking* movies, bringing him back into the mainstream, while his role in Quentin Tarantino's *Pulp Fiction* in 1994 would be hailed as his big comeback.

ABOVE: Lotus Formula One chief Colin Chapman gets some feedback from driver Mario Andretti after a practice session at Silverstone. Lotus led the 1978 competition with a superior car—its innovative 78 model, the first to employ the "ground effect" principle. Andretti won the Drivers' Championship and Lotus took the Constructors' Prize.

OPPOSITE: Demand for fitness equipment had begun to grow in the 1960s and during the early 1970s NASA had invested in developing treadmills, viewing them as a way of helping astonauts stay fit while in space. By the end of the decade keeping fit was fashionable but the craze really took off at the beginning of the 1980s with a rush of celebrity fitness videos.

ABOVE: Jack Nicholson with Australian actress Lyndall Hobbs. In 1978 Jack Nicholson was to turn his hand to directing, making and starring in the western *Goin' South*, a sentimental, gently humoros drama. Two years later he was to star in Stanley Kubrick's chilling horror *The Shining*, with Shelley Duvall, creating one of his most memorable characters in Jack Torrence.

OPPOSITE: Christopher Reeve had worked in theater and TV before landing the lead in 1978's hugely popular *Superman: The Movie*, and although he subsequently appeared in several other films, it is the role of Superman, in the original and its three sequels, for which Reeve will be best remembered. Reeve, a keen horseman, would fall while eventing and become paraplegic in 1995, losing his tenacious battle for life in 2004 after being wheelchair-bound and supported by breathing apparatus for nearly ten years.

1979

The coffin of Admiral of the Fleet Earl Mountbatten of Burma, draped with the Union Jack flag, lies in state in Westminster Abbey, London, on September 5. Mountbatten was enjoying a boat trip in Sligo Bay, Ireland, with some of his family, when the boat was blown up by an IRA bomb. His 14-year-old grandson, Nicholas, was also among those killed in the blast. The Queen and several members of the royal family were present at the funeral. Lord Mountbatten was a great-grandson of Queen Victoria and so related to both the Queen (seated right) and Prince Philip as well as being a mentor to Prince Charles.

Barry Manilow started out as a journeyman musician, playing piano and writing jingles. His student days at the Juillard School combined with his natural talent helped his career develop, and when he started a collaboration with Bette Midler, his own solo career took off with "Mandy" in 1974. By 1978 he had a string of hits to his name and in that year five albums simultaneously in the charts.

The Police, messing about by the River Thames at Putney. Sting, left, and Stewart Copeland, standing right, are about to launch Andy Summers into the water. The Police adapted a reggae and punk flavor to their own unique style; their chart career took off with the single "Roxanne," taken from their first album, *Outlandos d'Amour*, released in 1978.

1979

RIGHT: Conservative Party leader Margaret Thatcher pictured speaking at a conference in 1979. In the foreground are the now famous "Labour Isn't Working" posters, designed by advertising agency Saatchi and Saatchi. Over the winter of 1978–79, popularly referred to as the "Winter of Discontent," the Labour Government was facing harsh criticism against a background of spiraling unemployment, industrial action, and the collapse of public services.

OPPOSITE: The remains of the car belonging to member of parliament Airey Neave, who was killed by a car bomb as he left the House of Commons car park in March 1979. Neave died from his injuries at Westminster Hospital. Both the IRA and the Irish National Liberation Army claimed responsibility for the attack, although it was later suggested that the assassination was carried out by British or American intelligence agents, either due to Neave's plans to overhaul the security services, and in doing so expose corruption, or on account of his policy toward Northern Ireland.

ABOVE: Members of the British comedy team Monty Python during the filming of their controversial film *Life of Brian* (from left): John Cleese as Centurion of the Yard, Michael Palin as Pontius Pilate, and Graham Chapman as Biggus Dickus. The movie was a box office success both sides of the Atlantic but its religious satire was too much for some people. When EMI Films withdrew backing a few days before production began, George Harrison stepped in with Handmade Films and filled the £3 million funding gap.

OPPOSITE: Leonard Nimoy as Vulcan science officer Spock, and William Shatner as Admiral James T. Kirk, former captain of the *SS Enterprise* and now a commander at Starfleet HQ, seen here in a still from *Star Trek: The Motion Picture*. In this rather uncharacteristic situation for the Vulcan, Kirk is visiting his sickbay bed after Spock has been wounded by an alien incursion.

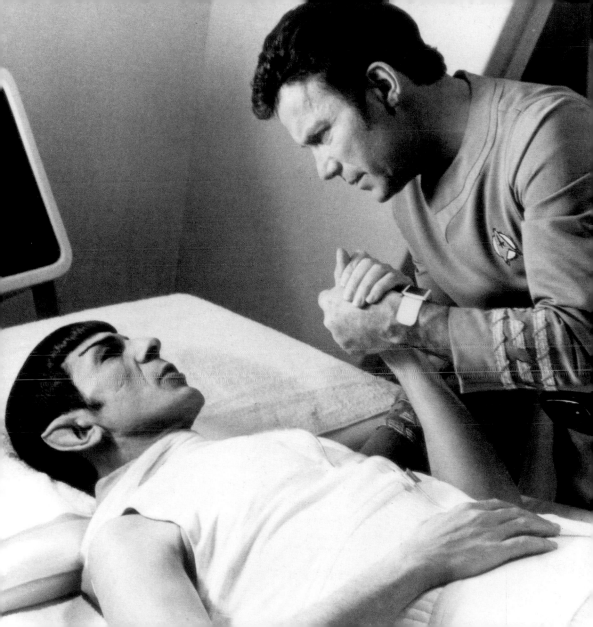

1979

ABOVE: In February 1979 Queen Elizabeth embarked on a tour of the Arabian Gulf, flying out on Concorde with David Owen, British Foreign Secretary (left). Britain had a long history with the Gulf States and generally their rulers had a cordial relationship with the UK. However, behind the royal visit was the need to secure Britain's relationship with the oil producing countries that formed OPEC, especially in the context of increasing instability in the Middle East.

OPPOSITE: A Russian personnel carrier moving through the Salang Pass in Afghanistan. The Russians invaded Afghanistan on Christmas Eve, 1979: for them it was to be a long, bitter, and ultimately fruitless invasion. The Afghan Mujaheddin, financed by the USA, fought back continuously and mercilessly. Eventually, the bitterness of it all—the people, the weather, and the terrain—would get the better of Russia, forcing them to withdraw.

1979

ABOVE: The cast of *Fawlty Towers*, BBC TV's highly successful comedy series, from left to right: Prunella Scales, Connie Booth, John Cleese, and Andrew Sachs. John Cleese and Connie Booth, who at the time the show started in 1975 were married, wrote the scripts centered around eccentric halfwit hotel owner Basil Fawlty, Cleese's slapstick creation, set in a tired and clichéd hotel on England's south coast. Only 12 episodes were made over two seasons and the final episode was screened in October 1979.

OPPOSITE: Rock group Pink Floyd rehearse prior to a concert. At the end of November Pink Floyd released their album *The Wall*, which went to the top of the *Billboard* album chart, staying there for 15 weeks. The band toured *The Wall* with a spectacular stage show; Alan Parker was hired to direct a feature film based on the tour, also called *The Wall*, which would eventually be released in 1982.

1979

ABOVE: Egyptian President Anwar Sadat, US President Carter, and Israeli Prime Minister Menachem Begin clasp hands on the White House lawn, after Egypt and Israel signed a historic peace agreement in March. Egypt was the first Arab nation to even enter into talks with Israel, and although the move was not universally popular, particularly in Palestine, Sadat and Begin were awarded the Nobel Peace Prize as a result of their efforts to bring stability to the Middle East.

OPPOSITE: Margaret Thatcher with her husband Denis on the steps of 10 Downing Street. On May 4, 1979, Thatcher became Britain's first female prime minister, the Conservative Party having won a decisive victory in the general election. Callaghan's Labour government fell after a vote of no confidence. In the election the Conservatives went on to gain almost 43 percent of the national vote, taking 61 seats directly from Labour, to secure a total of 339 seats, giving a substantial majority of 44 seats in the House of Commons.

ABOVE: Martin Sheen starring in the 1979 movie *Apocalypse Now*. In addition to the natural obstacles of filming in tropical conditions with bad weather that wrecked sets, the pressure felt by both the production team and the actors caused serious psychological problems. Coppola's work on this movie can be summed up by the word "excess:" it took years to make, and Coppola shot so much film that editing was as much of a challenge as the actual filming.

OPPOSITE: Tom Skerrit, Harry Dean Stanton, and Veronica Cartwright in a scene from Ridley Scott's sci-fi horror movie *Alien*. A relatively low-budget movie, shot in 14 weeks, *Alien* is generally recognized as a masterpiece of cinema. Scott's attention to detail, his mastery of camera and lighting, the integration of high-quality design for every aspect, plus brilliant casting and plot made a stunning film and a massive box office success for it and its five sequels.

RIGHT: Niki Lauda won the Formula One championship in 1975, 1977, and 1984, showing great courage in returning to racing after his horrific Nürburgring injury in 1976. However, after a dismal year with team Brabham, in a totally uncompetitive car, Lauda decided he'd had enough, walking out at Montreal, the penultimate race of the season.

OPPOSITE: John McEnroe won his first Grand Slam title, the US Open, in 1979 and this launched his championship career, which would see a further three US Open wins and three Wimbledon singles championships. A volatile personality on the court, McEnroe became notorious for overstepping the mark with umpires and making competition with the likes of Borg and Connors into something of a feud.

1979

LEFT: The latest thing in home entertainment—a video recorder. Sony's Betamax format was launched in 1975 for the domestic market but JVC introduced its VHS format in 1977. The ensuing format war went on for over a decade until Sony released their own VHS-based machines. Although targeting the home user, the recorders were still expensive, which led to a boom in the home rental market until prices became more affordable. The video cassette recorder or VCR was the first step in the transformation of the video entertainment market and it would soon become an essential piece of home equipment.

OPPOSITE: With the dawning of the home computing era electronic games became the latest trend. Naturally some of them appealed equally to fathers, with even the simplest games available for the Atari VCS proving quite addictive. Even the clever memory game Simon, launched in 1978, had a space-age console.

1979

RIGHT: An Iranian student supporter holds up a poster of Iran's new ruler, Ayatollah Ruhollah Khomeini, outside the American Embassy in London in November. Early in 1979 the Shah of Iran went into exile; a national referendum in the spring voted for Iran to become an Islamic Republic and Khomeini established a new constitution, appointing his prime minister. In November, a group of activist students, incensed by the Shah's arrival in the US for cancer treatment, occupied the US Embassy in Iran and held 52 of its staff hostage for over a year.

OPPOSITE: Hundreds of thousands of refugees fled Southeast Asia after the Communist takeover of Vietnam and the Khmer Rouge in Cambodia. They took to the sea in small boats and headed into the main shipping channels, hoping to be picked up by passing freighters. The lucky "Boat People," as they became known, ended up in the USA or other western countries. Others were lost at sea or robbed and murdered by pirates. Those that survived the journey were often detained in camps with miserable conditions while they waited to be given resident status.

1979

RIGHT: Singer Cliff Richard gives a cheery wave. In 1979 Richard scored a huge hit with the single "We Don't Talk Anymore," which was produced by the Shadows' Bruce Welch and featured Brian Ferry. Released in late 1979, the song reached number one in the UK and the top ten in the US. This made Richard the first artist to chart on the *Billboard* Hot 100 in the 1980s while also having scored Hot 100 hits in all of the previous three decades.

OPPOSITE: Penny Marshall (right) and Cindy Williams in *Laverne and Shirley*, the US TV sitcom that was one of a number of spin-offs from the long-running series *Happy Days*. The show broadcast 178 episodes on ABC TV between 1976 and 1983 and achieved top ratings; the story was set in the past, beginning 1959 and ending 1967. Filmed in the Paramount studio next to *Happy Days*, there were frequent guest appearances between the two shows.

1979

OPPOSITE: Amid the ruins of their war-torn city, Beirut residents and tourists take advantage of a lull in the fighting to go swimming in the Mediterranean Sea in the summer of 1979. While Israel had secured stable peace with Egypt and had its Syrian enemies under control, its northern neighbor, Lebanon, provided the base for terrorist incursions. Lebanon became the melting point of the Middle East Crisis from 1975 to 1990, its own civil war fueled by external interests around the world.

ABOVE: Still one of the most eligible bachelors in the world, Prince Charles talks to polo club secretary Jane Ward.

1979

March 26: Magic Johnson of the Michigan State University Spartans, looks for an open man against number 33 Larry Bird of the Indiana State University Sycamores in Salt Lake City, Utah on March 26.

OPPOSITE: Bob Geldof and his girlfriend Paula Yates at the premiere of the film *Quadrophenia*, which was based on The Who's rock opera of the same name. In 1979 Geldof and his band, the Boomtown Rats, were propeled to fame by the number one single "I Don't Like Mondays," which was controversially inspired by the actions of 16-year-old Brenda Ann Spencer, who went on a shooting spree at Cleveland Elementary School in California in January 1979, killing two adults and injuring several children.

RIGHT: John Lydon, a.k.a Johnny Rotten, pictured outside court in 1979. Following the disbandment of the Sex Pistols, Lydon initiated legal proceedings against former manager Malcom McLaren, with the hearings beginning just days after bassist Sid Vicious had died of a heroin overdose in New York. At the same time, Lydon was enjoying success with his new group, Public Image Ltd. alongside bass player Jah Wobble and former Clash guitarist Keith Levene.

1979

LEFT: Richard Kiel as Jaws and Blanche Ravalec as his newfound love in *Moonraker*, the latest James Bond movie. The movie was expensive to make by previous standards but performed well at the box office: it was the 11th Bond movie of the franchise and Roger Moore's fourth in the leading role.

OPPOSITE: Michael Douglas (left) and Jane Fonda attend to Jack Lemmon, who has been shot at the climax of movie *The China Syndrome*. Centered on dangerous irregularities at a nuclear power station, the movie achieved critical recognition, winning Best Actor for Jack Lemmon at the Academy Awards and the Palme d'Or at Cannes. In a bizarre coincidence, just a few days after the release of the movie there was an accident at the Three Mile Island Nuclear Generating Station in Pennsylvania which brought the issues in the movie into sharp relief.

1979

ABOVE: (Left to right) Bishop Abel Mizarewa, Lord Carrington (British Foreign Secretary), Sir Ian Gilmour, Joshua Nkomo, and Robert Mugabe at the signing ceremony of the Anglo-Zimbabwe Conference at Lancaster House, London. In 1965 Ian Smith had issued a unilateral declaration of independence, seceding Southern Rhodesia from UK dependency. This was not recognized by either the UK or the UN and economic sanctions ensued. As well as external pressure, Smith's white minority government struggled to control militant dissenters. Ultimately Ian Smith had little choice: he made an internal settlement in 1979, resulting in a coalition government headed by Mizarewa, and this was followed by the Lancaster House Agreement. In 1980 the legally independent state of Zimbabwe came into being with Robert Mugabe as prime minister.

OPPOSITE: Crowds carrying banners at a demonstration during the Rhodesia crisis.

At 4:00 a.m. on March 29, radioactive steam leaked from the Three Mile Island Nuclear Generating Station in Dauphin County, Pennsylvania. It was the most serious accident in the history of US commercial nuclear power plant operations. Following the accident, the nuclear plant building program in the US was halted.

ACKNOWLEDGMENTS

Written and edited by:
Tim Hill; Gareth Thomas; Murray Mahon; Marie Clayton; Duncan Hill; Jane Benn; Alison Gauntlett; Alice Hill

****

The photographs in this book are from the archives of the *Daily Mail*. Thanks to all the photographers who have contributed and the film and television companies who have provided Associated Newspapers with promotional stills.
Every effort has been made to correctly credit photographs provided. In case of inaccuracies or errors we will be happy to correct them in future printings of this book.

Thanks to all the staff at Associated Newspapers who have made this book possible. Particular thanks to Alan Pinnock.
Thanks also to Steve Torrington, Dave Sheppard and Brian Jackson.

Thanks to the many Associated Newspapers photographers who have contributed including: B Greenwood, Ray Brigden, Phillip Jackson, James Gray, Edwin Sampson, Bill Cross, Stilling, Norman Potter Michael Brennan, Monty Fresco, John Walters, Aylott, Laurie Asprey, Graham Wood, Geoffrey White, John Sherbourne, Smart,
Clive Limpkin, Dempsie, David Thorpe, Tim Graham, Nick Rogers, Howard, Mike Hollist, Jeff Morris, Jim Hutchison, Brian Bould, Neville Marriner, Johnson, Potter, Ken Towner, Ling, Thorpe, Roger Allston, Hart, James, Tony Weaver,
With contributions from associated photographers: Serge Moritz, Kurt Strumpf, Charles Tasnadi, Neal Ulevich, Heng Sinith, Jean-Pierre Prevel, Bob Daugherty,

Additional photographs courtesy Getty Images
Focus On Sport, Getty Images North America pg 12 pg 35 pg 116-117 pg 125 pg 160-161 pg 173 pg 260; Popperfoto/Getty Images pg 26; AFP/Getty Images pg 99 pg 380-381; Arthur Jones, Getty Images, Hulton Archive pg 114; Tony Tomsic, Getty Images North America pg 138; RacingOne/Getty Images pg 210; John Minihan, Getty Images pg 283 pg 290; Fotos International, Getty Images pg 368; Michael Ochs Archives pg 42

NASA: page 247 courtesy of NASA

Film and Television

The Railway Children, EMI Film Productions 24; Get Carter, Metro-Goldwyn-Mayer 29; Diamonds Are Forever, United Artists/Eon Productions 54; The French Connection, Twentieth Century Fox 55; The Last Picture Show, Columbia Pictures 60; The Candidate, Warner Bros. 93; Last Tango in Paris, United Artists 94; Carry On Matron, Anglo Amalgamated 109; The Godfather, Paramount Pictures 112; Papillon, Allied Artists Pictures/Columbia Pictures 118; The Way We Were, Columbia Pictures 123; A Touch of Class, Avco/Brut Productions 129; The Great Gatsby, Paramount Pictures 195, Shamus, Columbia Pictures 196; Shampoo, Columbia Tristar 198-99; The Return of the Pink Panther, United Artists 227; Bugsy Malone, Rank 273; Annie Hall, United Artists 274- 275; Star Wars, United Artists/Lucasfilm 300; The Spy Who Loved Me, United Artists/Eon Productions 302; The Deer Hunter, EMI Films 309; Coma, Metro-Goldwyn-Mayer 331; Monty Python's Life of Brian, Warner Bros./Orion Pictures/HandMade Films 352; Star Trek: The Motion Picture, Paramount Pictures 353; Apocalypse Now, United Artists 360; Alien, Twentieth Century Fox 361; The China Syndrome, Columbia Tristar 377; Steptoe and Son, Associated London Films 28; All in the Family, Bud Yorkin Productions/CBS Television 76- 77; Ironside, Harbour Productions Limited 82; Colditz, BBC 83; Are You Being Served?, BBC 90; Alias Smith & Jones, Universal TV 133; Whatever Happened to the Likely Lads?, BBC 142; Columbo, NBC 143; Some Mothers Do 'Ave 'Em, BBC 147; Upstairs Downstairs, LWT 170; The Waltons, BBC 186; Happy Days, Paramount Television/ABC 191; The Six Million Dollar Man, ABC/MCA 194; Tiswas, ATV/ITV 208; Porridge, BBC 224; The Good Life, BBC 225; Police Story, BBC 226; Starsky and Hutch, Spelling-Goldberg Productions 242; Sesame Street, CTW/Jim Henson Productions/Sesame Workshop/PBS 243; Charlie's Angels, Spelling-Goldberg Productions 250; The Fall and Rise of Reginald Perrin, BBC 251; Rock Follies, Thames Television 265; Roots, BBC 281; The Morcambe and Wise Christmas Show, BBC 289; The Muppet Show, ATV/ITV 312; Rising Damp, Yorkshire Television 328; The Two Ronnies, BBC 329; Multi-Coloured Swap Shop, BBC 336; The Rockford Files, Cherokee Productions 337 Fawlty Towers, BBC 356; Laverne and Shirley, Paramount Television/Henderson Productions/ Miller-Milkis Productions 368; The New Avengers, The Avengers Enterprises/ITV 256

Published by Transatlantic Press
First published in 2010

Transatlantic Press
38 Copthorne Road
Croxley Green, Hertfordshire
WD3 4AQ

© Atlantic Publishing
For photograph copyrights see pages 382–3

A catalogue record for this book is available from the British Library.

ISBN 978-1-907176-01-2

Printed in China